the
newlywed's
instruction
manual

the
newlywed's
instruction manual

ESSENTIAL INFORMATION, TROUBLESHOOTING TIPS,
AND ADVICE FOR THE FIRST YEAR OF MARRIAGE

by Caroline Tiger

Illustrated by Paul Kepple and Scotty Reifsnyder

QUIRK BOOKS
PHILADELPHIA

Copyright © 2010 by Quirk Productions, Inc.

Library of Congress Cataloging in Publication Number: 2009940385

ISBN: 978-1-59474-436-5

Printed in China

Typeset in Swiss

Designed and illustrated by Paul Kepple and Scotty Reifsnyder @ Headcase Design
    www.headcasedesign.com
Edited by Sarah O'Brien
Production management by John J. McGurk

10

Quirk Books
215 Church Street
Philadelphia, PA 19106
quirkbooks.com

Contents

Congratulations!

ATTENTION!

If you're reading this book, there's a good chance you have recently been married. Congratulations on surviving the wedding—the guests, the caterer, the in-laws, the flowers, the music, the reception, the stress, and the bill. But as much as the wedding day may overshadow marriage itself, don't forget that the real point is what comes after. If this fact slipped your mind throughout the entire wedding process, we're here to remind you: You are officially married. Now what?

The notion of "happily ever after," popularized by many pop-cultural sources but especially by Jane Austen novels and their movie adaptations, is a common one. It implies that the struggle is all in the courtship. Once the couple weds, the cliché goes, they are destined for unsullied happiness and all their problems will disappear. In reality, newlywed life more resembles the writings of another nineteenth-century scribe, Charles Dickens, who famously penned, "It was the best of times. It was the worst of times . . . it was the spring of hope, it was the winter of despair."

To express the degree of difficulty in being a newlywed, it may help to compare it to another harrowing undertaking that's fresh in your mind: planning the wedding. That was a walk in the park compared to this. You're conditioned to think otherwise based on the reams of material that exist on how to plan a wedding. In fact, the difficulty of planning a wedding is inversely proportional to the number of books written and reality shows produced around wedding-planning how-tos.

In fact, most experts agree that the first year of marriage is the hardest. Why, you ask? Many reasons: You're getting used to each other. You're laying a foundation for the way your marriage will operate. You're learning when to compromise, how to negotiate differences, how to handle your in-laws, and all of the other aspects that go into your new life as a pair. You are no longer operating solo. Most newlyweds joke about the moment that occurs soon after returning from the honeymoon when they see their partner's dirty socks on the floor and reality hits them like a ton of bricks: "This is my life. These are my dirty socks on the floor. Forever." It helps to be able to find the humor in that daunting notion, and it helps to have a manual.

The Newlywed's Instruction Manual is meant to be a guide to the post-wedding period, when the fairy dust has been swept away and what's left are two saucer-eyed kids and a pile of presents to return. This guide will help with the myriad topics that come up during the first year—including merging finances, deciding where to spend the holidays, decorating the house on a budget (and with two styles to accommodate), practicing healthy communication, maintaining the romance, and many others. This manual does not purport to suggest that you should have everything figured out by the time you're no longer a newlywed. But it will help you make a dent in the meatier matters and give you the tools for navigating this time of extremes, this tale of two cities.

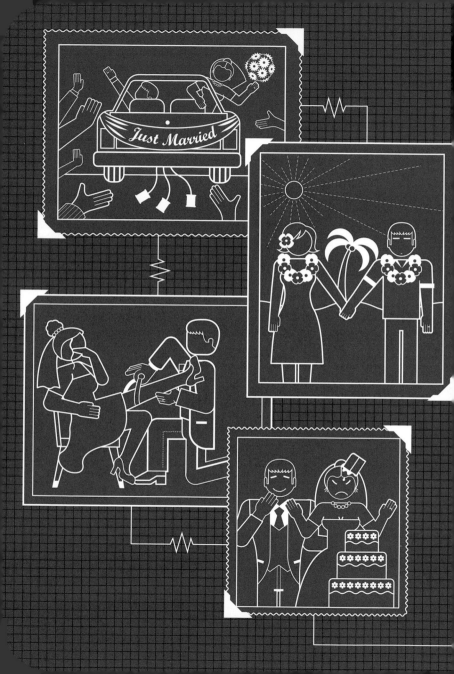

[Chapter 1]

Post-Wedding

After the Honeymoon

You didn't have any time to tie up loose ends during the weeks before the wedding and had even less time to do so between the reception and the honeymoon. So there are a few things to take care of upon your return. Here are suggested steps to completing some of the more complicated tasks.

Thank-You Notes for Gifts

If you didn't get these done on the long flight to Hawaii/Australia/Anguilla, you're going to have to take care of them soon after your return from the honeymoon. Despite what you've heard, you don't have a year to write thank-you notes. They should be written within two weeks of the gift's receipt. (And your guests shouldn't take a year to send their gift, either, but that's a different book.) It's tempting to put off writing thank-you notes when you're staring down a gargantuan pile of presents and gift envelopes, but take heed of the maxim: One bite at a time. In this case, the cliché is golden.

Who Should Write Them?

Splitting up the list makes it more manageable and has the added benefit of setting the tone for the highly evolved, egalitarian marriage of every newlywed's dreams. The bride takes on the writing of her own family's notes and the groom assumes his. The same goes for work friends and colleagues and for social friends. If there are guests who don't belong more to one side than the other, they can be split down the middle.

⚠️ **Exception:** *Thank-you notes should always, always be handwritten. So, if one of you has illegible handwriting, it's unfortunately up to the other to take on the burden of the note-writing.*

Who Should Sign Them?

It's a nice touch for both newlyweds to sign each note. Doing so lets the recipient know that you are equally invested in cherishing the bone-china soup tureen or the lovely set of kitchen towels. If it isn't practical, one signature per thank-you note is perfectly acceptable.

The Tools

Pen: Choose a pen that's quick drying and nonsmudging; blue or black ink is best. (Green, red, and silver ink should be reserved for holiday notes or for those written by persons under the age of thirteen.)

Paper: Thank-you notes that match the wedding stationery are very lovely. Often a proactive bride has thought ahead and purchased matching stationery. Even more often, however, the newlyweds are out of money and ideas, exhausted from being bled dry by the wedding-industrial complex, and they opt to purchase relatively inexpensive, generic notecards. By now, the bride is likely to reason that most wedding guests aren't likely to notice efforts at coordination and matchiness, so why spend the extra money and time? Yes, newlyweds can be a little jaded.

Attitude: Adopt a thankful one. Clear your head so that you can think about each gift and formulate a personalized sentiment regarding the item and your relationship with the person who offered it.

The Basic Format

- Greeting.
- Mention the gift right away.
- Personalize the note by saying how you feel about the person and the gift. (Prompts: Why do you like it? How will you use it? When will you use it?)
- Say "thank you."
- Wind down.
- Close.

FOLD HERE

FOLD HERE

Dear Joan and Phil,

Thank you so much for the beautiful vase you gave us for our wedding. We put it on our kitchen table and fill it with

fresh-cut flowers every week. Thanks for sharing our special day. Hope to see you soon!

Love,
Amanda and Jim

FIRST CLASS

Troubleshooting

If you don't like the gift . . .

Lie, unless you're guaranteed to be found out. For example, if your spouse's aunt and uncle who live down the street gave you an intricately carved, four-poster bed that's been in the family forever, they're likely to notice if you're not using it.

If you're not sure whether their card is the gift or if they're sending a "real" gift later . . .

Send a thank-you note that thanks them for coming to the wedding and for their card's lovely sentiments. If they send a gift later, too, send another note for that.

If you're not sure whether you already sent a thank-you note . . .
This pesky "if" underscores the importance of keeping track. There are many handy online tools for brides and grooms/newlyweds to keep track of who sent a gift and who has received a thank-you note.

Troubleshooting Gifts

There's a reason couples go through the bother of creating registries, but many guests still feel the need to do something more personal. This is fine if your guests know your taste, but if they don't, some issues may arise. Then there are those guests who don't give any gift. Here are some guidelines for dealing with these situations.

"Gone Missing"

This is what you call the gifts that are still missing in action six months after the wedding. You reason aloud to your friends and your hair stylist that you certainly didn't have a wedding just to get gifts. After all, what kind of coarse brute thinks of a gift as the price of admission to a blessed event celebrating the union of two souls? But to each other and to yourselves, you wonder about the chutzpah of people who don't realize that a gift is the price of admission to a wedding and that they should've calculated the per-plate cost at the reception and selected a present accordingly.

Who Hasn't Given You a Gift and Wh

■ **WHO:** The twenty-something cousin

■ **WHY:** Just clueless

■ **WHO:** Groom's old college friend

■ **WHY:** Groom never sent him a gift when he got married

The best way to deal with such situations is to let it go and be thankful for the wonderful gifts you did receive. In the big picture, a few extra presents won't make much of a difference anyway.

WHO: The great uncle, once removed

WHY: Have a heart. He's on a fixed budget.

■ **WHO:** The couple you socialize with infrequently

■ **WHY:** They kept meaning to, but they never got around to it and then they just forgot. They'll remember when they see you next. It'll be awkward.

How to Return Gifts Without Receipts

Although no one has done a survey to determine the percentage of wedding gifts the average couple returns or exchanges, the number probably hovers somewhere around 25 percent. There's no reason to assume you're obligated to keep something if you don't like it or have no use for it. Of course, there are always a few gifts that are impossible to return, specifically the handmade and personalized items. (The chances of another couple whose last name starts with "Z" is low.)

Since gifts are not guaranteed to come with gift receipts or from a registry, returning them can be tricky. Here are some tips to ensure success at unloading the duplicates or the uglies and receiving store credit:

■ Check that the item is still available at the store. If it's not, the clerk will be less likely to take it back. (This is an incentive for returning items without delay.)

■ Frame the return as an exchange. Decide in advance what you'd like so you can approach the clerk not with a negative (a return) but with a positive: "I'd like to exchange this Provençal serving dish for the 12-inch stick blender, please."

■ Say *please* and *thank you*. Working retail is difficult. Sales associates are more likely to accommodate you if you're pleasant and appreciative.

■ Pick the day strategically. Right after the winter holidays, stores are less likely to put up resistance. If you don't mind waiting in longer lines, those times are a good bet.

Expert Tip: *In most cases, you should still write a thank-you note for a gift you plan to return or have already returned. The exception is if you've received duplicates and have decided to exchange one for something else on the registry. You can disclose this fact in the note since it indicates that you did appreciate the original gift.*

All That Wedding Stuff

During months of wedding planning, the stuff piles up. Then it piles up on top of the initial pile. There is stuff galore: wedding magazines, crafting supplies (if you're the DIY type), leftover favors and menus and programs, wedding books, extra envelopes, swatches of fabric, unused centerpiece vases, etc. Chances are that these items are taking up valuable real estate in your teeny, tiny apartment.

Even if a recent bride doesn't feel ready to let go of her dress, even if tossing the leftover programs feels sacrilegious to you both, ask yourself if you'll ever really use or look at these things again. Why not save one example for your scrapbook and toss the rest? Ask yourself how it'll feel (a) to recoup some of the money you spent on your dress and (b) to know that some other bride-to-be will have the day of her life in that dress, too. Why not bring it to a consignment shop instead of letting it gather dust, boxed up in your basement? Your programs are made of paper. Recycle those, too.

In addition to bridal consignment shops, there are many Web sites where you can sell gently used wedding décor and apparel. Do it. Clear the clutter from one phase of life to psychically and physically clear your space for the next phase: newlywed-ness.

What to Keep and What to Give Away

Keep:

- Guest book
- One or two invitations
- One or two programs
- One or two menus
- Shoes and accessories
- Gocco machine (for screenprinting)
- Xyron machine (for laminating and sticker-making)

Sell/Give Away/Throw Away:

■ Card box (sell online or toss, depending on condition and prettiness)

■ Table numbers (sell online)

■ Menus (toss)

■ Placecards (toss)

■ The dress (consignment shop)

■ The veil (consignment shop)

■ Overtly bridal accessories, including sparkly hairclips for updos and ivory clutches (sell online)

■ Centerpiece/tabletop materials, including vases, runners (sell online)

■ Candy buffet items (sell online)

What to Keep/Toss from the Wedding Binder/Box/Folder/Notes:

■ Address lists (keep electronically)

■ Tear sheets with wedding apparel or décor ideas (toss)

■ Inspiration boards (toss)

■ Vendors' contracts (keep for three months, then toss)

■ Samples of table linens, veil material, favors, etc. (toss)

■ Chart of guests' gifts and thank-you notes (keep electronically)

Where to Sell Online

Online classifieds work best when they're part of a popular wedding Web site with active forums. The Knot (theknot.com) has a forum especially for selling supplies and apparel, called Trash to Treasure. Weddingbee (weddingbee.com) also has a classifieds section. Ebay and Craigslist are good outlets, too. The latter has the added benefit of being local, which reduces shipping costs.

Preserving Your Dress
(If You Decide to Keep It)

Preservationists caution that you should clean and preserve your dress as soon as possible after the wedding. Wait too long and certain stains, like red wine, mud, or the soy-glaze from the fish entrée, can set permanently in satin and silk. Ask the shop where you purchased your bridal gown and/or recent brides in your area for preservationist referrals. It's important to use someone with a good track record because the delicate and sumptuous fabrics commonly used to construct wedding gowns require careful cleaning and storage methods. When you pick up the dress after treatment, it'll likely be boxed in an acid-free or pH-neutral paperboard box complete with a viewing window. If you're tempted to open the box and handle the dress, make sure your hands are clean. Store the box in a temperate room—not one that gets very hot, very cold, or at all damp. The cost of preservation can range from $200 to $800.

Preserving Your Tux or Suit

Lucky groom—you get to wear your tux or suit again and again. No mummifying of wedding duds for you. However, you should have it dry-cleaned when you return from your honeymoon. Chances are the wedding day was long—and sweaty.

The Difference Between You and Me

The first few years of married life are partly about discovering the differences between you and your partner and then figuring out how to negotiate these distinctions. The issue of clutter is bound to become a significant cause of strife if one partner is a pack rat and the other is a clean freak. (The terms *pack rat* and *clean freak* denote the two extremes on the spectrum. More often than not, people are not so extreme but display tendencies toward each type.) If you and your partner are not on the same page as far as how to handle clutter, see page 73 for suggestions on how to keep the peace.

Memorializing the Event

As with many well-intentioned and ambitious plans, the idea to make a scrapbook and a shadow box, to frame the best photos, to order photos for each member of the bridal party and albums for both sets of parents—all will likely fall by the wayside during the first year of marriage. Here are two reasons these projects are likely to lie fallow.

Wedding Burnout: Though the day itself exceeded expectations, you've had enough of the planning and plotting and pasting and primping to last a lifetime, or at least as much time as it took to plan the wedding. This equation is similar to the one that dictates how long it takes to get over a breakup: If you were dating for three years, it takes one and a half years to fully recover. Similarly, if you were planning the wedding for eighteen months, give yourself nine months before diving into keepsake projects.

Cash: The money is now flowing toward the purchase of a home or special projects intended to fluff the feathers of your current nest. In other words: Money is going toward the future, not the past.

KEEPSAKE PROJECTS

A few creative ways to immortalize the day two "to-bes" became two newlyweds:

SHADOW BOX

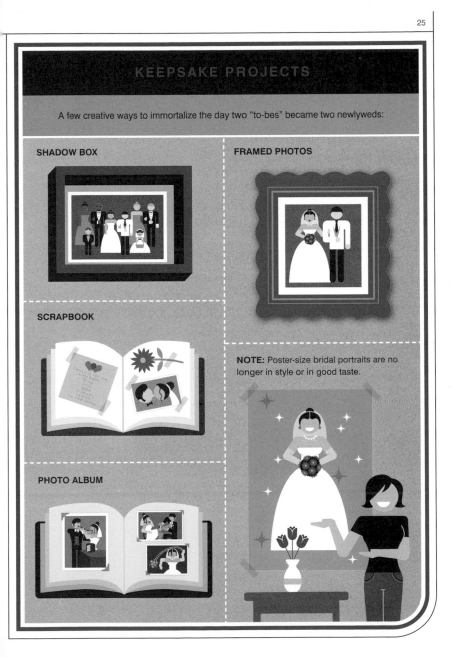

FRAMED PHOTOS

SCRAPBOOK

PHOTO ALBUM

NOTE: Poster-size bridal portraits are no longer in style or in good taste.

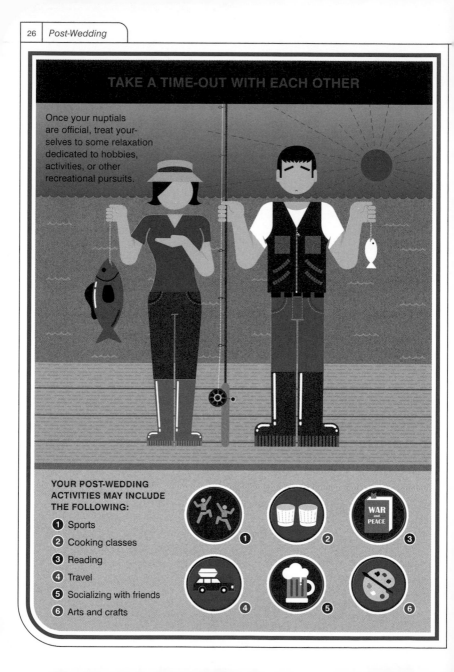

TAKE A TIME-OUT WITH EACH OTHER

Once your nuptials are official, treat yourselves to some relaxation dedicated to hobbies, activities, or other recreational pursuits.

YOUR POST-WEDDING ACTIVITIES MAY INCLUDE THE FOLLOWING:

1. Sports
2. Cooking classes
3. Reading
4. Travel
5. Socializing with friends
6. Arts and crafts

Free Time

Many engaged couples find that the months before the wedding are filled with wedding-related activities. Weekends are given over to wedding-related projects, and wistfully the to-bes look forward to a time when they can check off the activities on their "After the Wedding" (ATW) list.

That list might look something like this:

- Go fishing.
- Take cooking classes.
- Get the house back (meaning, free of wedding clutter).
- Visit friends and relatives who live in other states.
- Reserve leisurely Saturdays for doing absolutely nothing.
- Have the freedom to decide, on a whim, to take a Sunday drive somewhere new, and actually have the time to do it.
- Hang with friends on Monday nights at a favorite neighborhood bar.
- Switch from wedding blogs to home-design blogs.
- Work on artsy projects.
- Regain a social life.

So, it's over. Here's your chance. When the first weekend after the honeymoon arrives, you may find yourself growing antsy from nothing to do. Going through a big life-change is difficult, and that's true for this big shift from fiancés to newlyweds. Here's what to do: Consult your ATW list for ideas. If you didn't have an ATW list, write one now. Do it together.

Explore new hobbies, both individually and as a pair. It's as important to maintain your individuality as it is to find your identity as a couple. If you happen to be one of the newlyweds who suffers from PTWS (Post-Traumatic Wedding Syndrome), tackling this list will help fill the void.

Your Ring(s)

Your wedding band and/or engagement ring is probably the most expensive jewelry either of you have ever owned. They also happen to symbolize a very important union. It is, therefore, your large responsibility to keep them safe and sound. Your ring requires regular care and maintenance. Like a car or a kid, rings need to be checked every six months or so. This is especially true for engagement rings. Specifically, the setting needs to be eyeballed by a jeweler who'll make sure the stone hasn't come loose. After all, you don't want to lose your rock.

Insurance

You're extra-careful with your ring(s) and chances are nothing will ever happen to them, but it's important to have insurance just in case. Most insurance companies will add a rider (or an extension) to your homeowner's or renter's insurance policy to cover your wedding bands and/or engagement ring. These policies cover the items in your home up to a certain dollar value, and the rider allows you to increase the value that's covered. To secure a rider, you'll need receipts and appraisals, which you can request from the jeweler.

For the Ladies: Cleaning Your Engagement Ring

Most jewelers will let you come back as often as you'd like to get your engagement ring cleaned if your fiancé bought it from them. Take advantage of this service, since there's nothing like a good bath to make your diamond sparkle like it did on the day of your engagement.

ENGAGEMENT RING MAINTENANCE

With just a little care and maintenance, you can keep your ring looking as gorgeous as it did the day you got it.

KEEPING IT BEAUTIFUL:

1. Use a gentle dish detergent to clean buildup.

2. For extra shine, brush gently with a toothbrush after soaking in diluted ammonia.

REMOVE YOUR RING WHEN DOING THE FOLLOWING:

Working out

Preparing raw meat

Yardwork

If frequent trips to the jeweler aren't convenient, however, you can clean your ring at home using one of these methods:

■ Use a gentle dish detergent to clean buildup. Scrub the top and bottom with a soft toothbrush and rinse several times in hot water. For diamonds, you can use a drop of an all-purpose cleaner (such as Formula 409) with a large quantity of water, but be sure to rinse several times to remove all the cleaner. If you have an emerald ring, use only a gentle detergent; never use chemicals (such as Formula 409).

■ For extra shine, soak your diamond ring in a small bowl of ammonia diluted with three times the amount of water, and gently brush the top and bottom of the mounting with a soft toothbrush. Dip the ring into the solution again and then rinse it in warm water several times to be sure to remove all of the solution. Note: If you do this over an open drain, use a strainer! Set the ring on a soft towel to dry or gently pat it dry.

When and When Not to Wear

Sometimes you're concerned about mucking up your ring(s). Other times you may be concerned about it possibly slipping off and disappearing down a drain. As you get older, your fingers will grow in diameter, making it harder both to take off your ring(s) and for your ring(s) to slip off. Until then, you may want to think about when and when not to wear it.

Take it off before you . . .
■ **Handle raw meat.** This is the last thing you want stuck in a ring setting's nooks and crannies.

■ **Play sports.** Holding a racket (tennis, squash, or racquetball) tightly is not good for a wedding band that has stones set all the way around, especially if you're left-handed or have a two-handed backhand. As for wearing your ring(s) to the gym, lifting weights can be hazardous. You wouldn't want a 25-pound dumbbell making contact with the stone. (Then again, if your gym is full of single people looking to pick up their next date, you may want to leave it on.) If you're set on wearing your rings and you plan to lift weights, consider buying weightlifting gloves.

■ **Garden.** It's possible to chip a diamond or knock the setting loose while doing heavy yardwork.

■ **Clean.** Harsh chemical soaps or cleansers can soil ring(s). It's also a good idea to take off your ring(s) when washing dishes.

■ **Apply lotion, sunscreen, or perfume.** These products can leave a film on a diamond or other gemstone.

■ **Swim in the ocean or a pool.** You know how the ocean waters tend to shrink things? The same is true of your fingers, and the last place you want your ring(s) to get lost is in the deep blue sea. You may never find them again, at least not without the help of a professional diver. Also, pool chemicals can discolor gold and silver if exposed regularly over time. Platinum and titanium, on the other hand, can withstand most chemicals.

Keep it on when you're . . .

■ **Out for a drink with friends.** The ring should never come off when you're in a social situation and mingling with singles.

It can go either way if you're . . .

■ **Getting a massage.** You may want every inch of each finger available for massaging, and the therapist is likely to pull and knead less of your hand if you're wearing rings. Also, massage oils could loosen rings and increase the chance of them slipping off.

Safekeeping

Make sure to have a safe place to store your ring(s). Always travel with a dedicated ring box. Note that diamonds should be stored separately from other jewelry; they are extremely hard and can scratch other types of gemstones as well as metals.

At home it's a good idea to have ringholders stationed near the kitchen sink and on your bedroom dresser and anywhere else you're likely to remove your ring (a work table, the bathroom, etc.). Providing ease of storage means that you won't hastily place rings on the edge of some perilous precipice. Ringholders come in many forms and range from inexpensive to posh. In some parts of the country and in some families, a fancy ringholder is a common engagement gift. Some of these look like small trinket dishes; others are delicate boxes. The most useful kinds are in the shape of a hand with the fingers pointing up.

Your Spouse

Getting Used to Saying "Husband" and "Wife"

Some newlyweds claim that they feel "different" toward their spouse after the wedding. Others say they feel that neither they nor the relationship has changed much at all. This range of reactions probably has a lot to do with how long the couple was in a committed relationship prior to the wedding and whether or not they were living together. If a couple has been living together for many years, they may already feel married. However, one aspect of the relationship is guaranteed to change: that of their respective identities.

Girlfriend and boyfriend evolve to "fiancés," which transitions to "husband" and "wife." For the first six months or so, you're likely to stumble over these brand-new words just as, for the first few weeks after January 1, you stumble over the new year and still refer to it as the old one. It is human nature to need time to grow accustomed to such a primary change. If we didn't have a hard time with it, we'd be robots.

You'll probably notice it for the first time during the honeymoon, when hotel employees and others may ask about your husband or wife. Example: "Would you and your husband like the table by the pool or by the dance floor?" The first few times, you'll look around to see who the person is talking to before you realize that it's you: *You* are the wife or husband in question.

How Long Can You Call Yourselves "Newlyweds"?

There are several "official" answers floating around the universe, so you should feel free to choose the one that suits you best. Possible answers include

- One month
- One year
- Two years
- As long as you feel like newlyweds

Expert Tip: In common parlance, to "feel like newlyweds" means that you laugh together constantly, particularly at each other's jokes; stare at each other moony-eyed; and frequently act on the passionate feelings you have for each other. Don't feel bad if this does not describe you and your partner. The notion that a couple can maintain this fevered pitch of newlywed-ness over many years is largely mythical. It's much more typical to have newlywed-like moments scattered throughout a more even-keeled lifecycle.

Marriage Myths

To launch a successful marriage, it is imperative to clear away some commonly held notions that are more mythical than factual. It's not surprising that so many marriage-related myths pervade our society—most are propagated by the portrayal of marriages on television, in the movies, in literature, and by the public personas that many people present to the world when they describe their marriages as 100 percent perfect.

The average person doesn't have a large number of real-marriage role models. That is unfortunate, because these are what give you an idea of how marriage truly works. At most, there may be your own parents' marriage and maybe some other relatives' marriages (if they are close enough emotionally and geographically for you to observe their dynamics). Without real-life role models, you tend to put more stock in stereotypes.

Some common marriage myths debunked:

- **Myth:** Marriage is a cure-all for loneliness.
- **Reality:** Unfortunately, it's still possible to be lonely within a marriage.

- **Myth:** Marriage brings with it a guarantee of happiness ever after.
- **Reality:** A marriage cannot be your primary source of happiness. You need to be happy with yourself in order to be happy in your marriage.

- **Myth:** Being married makes you "complete."
- **Reality:** Although being married may add dimensions to your identity, it does not complete you. It's still up to you to complete yourself.

- **Myth:** Being married denotes instant adult status.
- **Reality:** No one becomes an adult instantly. You have to earn it.

- **Myth:** If you're truly meant for each other, your relationship/marriage will be easy.
- **Reality:** A good marriage comes from a willingness to work at the relationship, to compromise, and to constantly communicate. Doing so requires plenty of effort.

- **Myth:** Now that you're married, you'll be able to read each other's minds.
- **Reality:** A marriage license does not come with an ability to communicate telepathically. You still need to communicate more than ever about your needs, hopes, dreams, desires, and gripes.

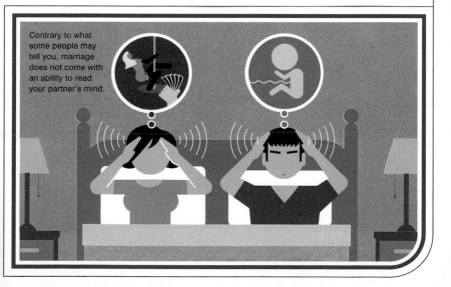

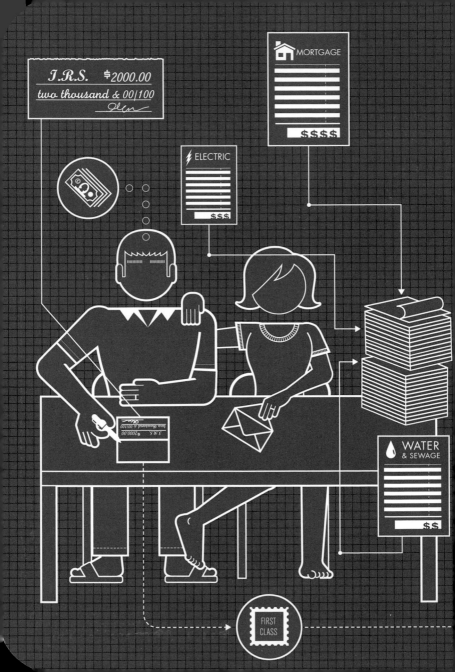

Chapter 2

Finances and Paperwork 101

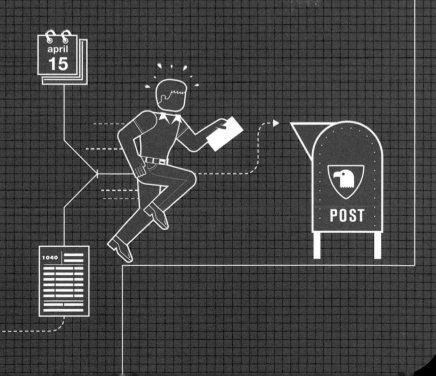

Now that your state and federal governments recognize you as a unit, it's time to extend that official state of affairs to the rest of your lives. There is plenty of dotting of *i*'s and crossing of *t*'s that needs to be accomplished before you are united in taxes, insurance, and bank accounts in addition to being united in body and spirit and before the eyes of whomever you chose to officiate your wedding.

Forms Beyond the Marriage License

Your family and friends know you've updated your marital status; now you need to inform the bureaucracies in your life. This involves the updating of many forms. Though it's certainly easier to leave them be, changes need to be made in order to enjoin the circumstances of yourself and your new spouse. Clear some time and store up some patience to take care of the following paperwork.

Sign up as each other's beneficiary. Check the beneficiary statements on your IRAs, employee pension plans, and life insurance policies. Your spouse should always be listed as the primary beneficiary.

Tweak insurance policies and titles. Review property, car, health, and life insurance policies to ensure that each of you is covered appropriately. Look at both of your health insurance policies and figure out which one works best for both of you. You may each end up staying on your pre-marriage policies, but you need to examine the options. Look at the differences in cost and treatment options, and, if you're switching, make sure your doctor is on your new plan.

If one of you earns much more money than the other, make sure the bigger earner has an airtight life insurance policy.

Also, if you haven't already reviewed the titles of property owned, such as cars, stock accounts, and real estate, do so now. You may want to title it in joint tenancy so that if one spouse dies, the surviving spouse is not disinherited.

Prepare for the worst. Write a simple will and durable powers of attorney for health and financial affairs. This ensures that if one spouse becomes disabled, the other is empowered to make the necessary decisions.

Changing Your Name(s)

Depending on the person, the decision to change your last name can range from easy to agonizing. This issue is commonly one that women face—men hardly ever change their names after marriage, although it's not unheard of. Below are the options, listed from most to least traditional, for newlyweds who are exploring a name change. Fictional couple Jane Smith and John Jones illustrate the choices:

- She takes his last name. (Jane and John Jones)
- She keeps her name. (Jane Smith)
- She adds his last name to hers, with or without a hyphen. (Jane Smith-Jones and John Jones)
- She keeps her name at work but takes his for social purposes. (Jane Smith at work; Jane Jones or Jane Smith-Jones everywhere else.)
- They each take the other's name, hyphenated or not (Jane Smith-Jones and John Jones-Smith)
- He takes her last name; she retains her name as is. (Jane and John Smith)

Reasons to Change

The most common reason is because changing your last name will make life easier. You won't need to bring your marriage certificate with you when you travel just in case your husband gets in an accident, is rushed to a hospital, and you need to prove that you are his wife in order to (a) visit him and/or (b) give consent for a procedure. Unfortunately, this worst-case scenario applies when you have children, too: No one will ask for proof that you're their mom if you share their last name. Less dire and more annoying are the stuck-in-the-past traditionalists to whom you'll need to continue to patiently explain that yes, these are your kids and, yes, you are married to that person even though you don't share the same last name.

Other reasons:

Tradition. At least when it comes to this decision, you are a traditionalist. You want to share a last name with the man you've married. You see this shared last name as a symbol of your united front. It makes you feel connected.

You hate your name. Your parents saw fit to name you Meredith Meredith, or you've been saddled your whole life with a surname that is the same as—or rhymes with—an embarrassing body part.

Reasons Not to Change

Your name is your identity. This reason often holds sway with women who marry later in life. When you've been known by a certain name for more than thirty years, you're likely to consider it to be an integral part of your identity. When you marry, you're not losing your identity, you reason, so why lose your name?

In your career, you're known by your name more than by your title or your affiliation with a company. If you're an artist—a performer, a writer, a musician—your name is your "brand," and it may set your career back to change it.

You're worried people won't be able to find you. There are people you knew earlier in life with whom you've lost touch, and you'd like them to be able to find you whenever they get around to looking.

You hate the other's name. It is the same as—or rhymes with—an embarrassing body part.

How to Change Your Name

Once you've decided to change your name, it's a good idea to do so soon after returning from your honeymoon. Get started right away because the changes need to filter through a series of bureaucratic venues, a process that always takes time. Here are the steps you need to take:

[1] Make sure you have your marriage certificate—the official one with the raised seal—because you'll need it as proof.

[**2**] Call the Social Security Administration's toll-free number. (Find it on www.ssa.gov.) An automated system will walk you through the name-change process. It's especially important for tax-filing purposes that your SSN matches your new name.

[**3**] Get a new driver's license with your new name by visiting the DMV, armed with your marriage certificate and a few other forms of photo identification. Remember to bring a book or a few magazines for the wait in the inevitably long, long line.

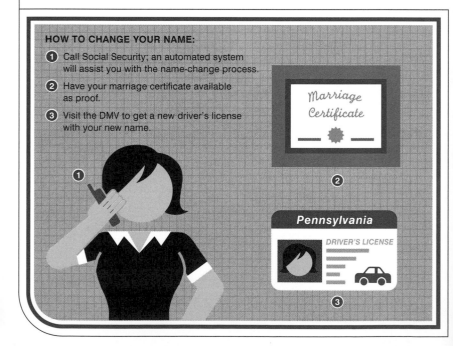

HOW TO CHANGE YOUR NAME:

1. Call Social Security; an automated system will assist you with the name-change process.
2. Have your marriage certificate available as proof.
3. Visit the DMV to get a new driver's license with your new name.

Marriage Certificate

Pennsylvania
DRIVER'S LICENSE

Change your name on the following documents:

- Passport (but not before the wedding; your name must match your maiden name if that's the one you used to book your travel plans)
- Mortgages and leases
- Wills
- Insurance policies

Don't forget to notify:

- Credit card companies
- Employers, for payroll and business cards
- The post office
- Phone and utility companies
- Banks
- Alumni associations
- Voter registration
- Magazines, for subscriptions

How to Let People Know About Your Decision

Because it's no longer predictable that once a woman marries she becomes Mrs. Hislastname, people will need guidance about what they're supposed to call you. Here are a few options:

With thank-you notes. The best way to let people know you have a new surname or that you're keeping your maiden name is to indicate it subtly via the return address on your thank-you note envelopes. You might consider getting a return address sticker or customized rubber stamp that you'll be able to use again and again.

In conversation. The first few times you're out with friends or family post-wedding, they may have occasion to introduce you to someone. You'll see them hesitate at, "I'd like you to meet my friends, John Jones and Jane, uh, ah . . . " Help them out and jump right in with the answer: "Jane Jones. Lovely to meet you" or "Jane Smith-Jones, lovely to meet you." Whatever, just clear the air.

By gentle correction. Whether or not you've changed your name, it'll take awhile for the new you or the new, old you to sink in for friends and acquaintances who have their own ideas about what's typical. Someone who expects every woman to change her name might continually introduce you—and send envelopes addressed to you—with your husband's last name, even if you didn't take it. The opposite is also true. There are sure to be slip-ups. Don't bulldoze the people who make them. Chances are they're innocent mistakes, not passive-aggressive commentary on your decision. Gently revise in conversation—"Actually I didn't take John's name. My name is still Jane Smith." And if you've received an envelope addressed incorrectly, simply bring it to that person's attention the next time you speak: "By the way, I didn't take John's name. My name is still 'Jane Smith.'"

Taxes

Once taxes are on the table, the honeymoon is really over. There are several concerns for newlyweds regarding the filing of taxes: Do you file jointly or separately? How do you decide? What kinds of tax benefits are you eligible for, if any, now that you're married? If you were married on or

HERE COMES THE TAXMAN!
To file jointly or not to file jointly: that is the question

REASONS TO FILE JOINTLY:

1 You will be eligible for more tax benefits and deductions.

2 The tax rates are lowest for joint returns.

before midnight of December 31 of the last tax year, you need to make some decisions as tax day looms.

Filing Jointly or Separately

Your choices are to file either a joint return or separate returns. Filing a joint return is called "Married Filing Jointly," and you'll combine your incomes and deduct all expenses on one tax return. If you file separate returns, it's called "Married Filing Separately." (Note: Most married couples file jointly since it gives them a bigger tax break.)

Reasons to file jointly:

■ It makes you eligible for more tax benefits and deductions, including those having to do with tuition and student loans.

■ The tax rates are lowest for joint returns.

Reasons to file separately:

■ Your combined income puts you in a higher tax bracket that requires you to pay more overall in taxes.

■ One of you is self-employed.

■ One of you owes child-support payments.

■ Your spouse tends to make "aggressive deductions," and you don't want to be liable if he or she is audited.

Merging Your Finances

Like most everything else, your finances have gone from a solo pursuit to a team sport. You're in it together now, and your first step (if you haven't already done so) needs to be a mutual airing of assets and debts. Inform each other of all checking and saving accounts, retirement funds, credit card debts, student or other loans, inherited property of significant worth, etc. Put everything on the table so that each person knows where you stand together as a couple. The next step is to come up with a plan for merging your finances.

Five Accounts

Most experts suggest maintaining five accounts (three joint and two individual). This allows you to set aside some liquid assets to pay for month-to-month expenses and to save for the long term on several different levels.

Here are the details:

■ Maintain the separate checking accounts opened before your marriage. Use these funds for personal expenses.

■ Open a joint checking account. You'll use this to pay household and other joint expenses. To know how much to deposit into this account every month, you'll need to determine your monthly budget. How much do you need, on average, to pay rent/mortgage, utilities, groceries, and payments on loans, cars, etc.? Now tally up the money needed for entertainment (dinners out, movies) in a typical month. Add them all and divvy up the total, according to your individual incomes.

■ Prorate the deposits so that the one who is earning more money will deposit more into the joint checking account. For example:

Husband's annual income: $145,000

Wife's annual income: $75,000

Monthly expenses: $1,600

The husband should deposit $1,066 (or 66%), and the wife should deposit $534 (or 33%) each month into the joint checking account.

Each partner should have three savings accounts (one individual and two joint)

■ A joint emergency fund with 3 to 6 months' worth of living expenses.

■ Each should have a retirement fund that you contribute to monthly or annually.

■ A savings/investment account for large, long-term goals, such as a down payment on a house, graduate school, the arrival of new family members, etc. Don't forget about this account because it's long-term. Keep an eye on it and treat yourselves with a dinner out when it reaches certain targets. This will keep you excited and motivated to continue to invest in the account (and will stop you from withdrawing monies from it).

Money Management

What's his is hers and what's hers is his. This adage really hits home once you realize that from now on you will each need to inform the other that you just made a big purchase, that your partner's school loans may as well be your own, and that you have now married someone else's credit score, for better or worse. These nitpicky details that come from merging finances are some of the reality sucker-punches that happen during the first few months of marriage.

Creating a Household Budget

Unless you're the type of person who always knows where each penny is going and is flush with cash for paying the bills, you need to think about creating a budget. And even if you are this type of person, you're now part of a unit made up of two people—and two people's spending habits. So your previous solo budget must be rehashed and reevaluated, with someone else in mind.

Wait two months. Since you're newly married, it's going to be hard to know how much you spend as a couple on daily expenses. During these two months, keep your receipts or write down where your daily dollars are going.

Acknowledge that drawing up a budget may be drudgery but is a necessary evil. Once the two months are up, make a date to go over what you've learned and use the information to create a budget. Lighten the chore by ordering pizza or promising yourselves a guilty-pleasure movie rental as soon as the deed is done.

Make three lists. Break down your spending into *fixed*, *variable*, and *miscellaneous* expenses. The first category includes expenses that are likely to be the same each month and that are not optional, such as the rent or mortgage, utilities, car loans, and health insurance. Variable expenses are everything else, including groceries, entertainment, transportation, pet care, and clothing. Put anything that doesn't fit into the first two categories under miscellaneous.

Add up your expenses. Based on your spending habits during the last two months, determine a monthly total for each subcategory within fixed, variable, and miscellaneous expenses.

CREATING A HOUSEHOLD BUDGET

Use this form to keep your budget in balance.

MONTHLY EXPENSES

FIXED:	VARIABLE:	MISC.:
Rent/mortgage $	Groceries $	$
Utilities $	Clothing $	$
School loan(s) $	Transportation $	$
Health insurance $	Credit card bills $	$
Cable/Internet $	Entertainment $	$
Car insurance $	Phone $	$
$	$	$

Monthly deposit to savings/retirement account $

FIXED ➕ VARIABLE ➕ MISC. ➕ SAVINGS ＝ $

TOTAL EXPENSES

MONTHLY INCOME

HIS:	HERS:	MISC.:
$	$	$

HIS ✚ HERS ✚ MISC. ═ $

TOTAL INCOME

TOTAL INCOME ━ TOTAL EXPENSES ═ $

TOTAL INCOME IS *LESS THAN* TOTAL EXPENSES:
Oh no! You must cut costs from your expenses to balance your budget.

TOTAL INCOME IS *GREATER THAN* TOTAL EXPENSES:
Congratulations on a job well done! Your budget is balanced.

DIGGING YOURSELF OUT OF DEBT

If your finances are in the red, here are a few ways to save money.

- ◯ Carpool to the office.
- ◯ Consolidate phone, Internet, and cable services.
- ◯ Negotiate with service companies.
- ◯ Insulate and reduce the thermostat.
- ◯ Forgo lavish gifts.
- ◯ Keep a communal coin jar.
- ◯ Install a water filter.
- ◯ Pack homemade lunches.
- ◯ Dine in rather than out.

Establish your savings objectives. Decide how much you should deposit into your savings accounts each month (or each paycheck) to reach long-term goals and contribute to retirement savings.

Note income. List all income sources in your household, including salaries (after taxes) and any other profit centers, such as eBay profits and poker winnings. Compare total income to total expenses plus total savings objectives. If the former is greater than the latter, things are not so bad. If the latter is greater than the former, you'll need to eliminate some costs from the budget.

Trimming the Fat and Dealing with Debt

Getting out of debt should be your top priority, because it'll be difficult to move ahead with any significant plans while you're still paying for long-gone shopping sprees. Besides, large debts pull down your credit scores, and those are vital to obtaining a favorable mortgage rate when you get around to house-hunting.

Even if you're not in debt, you should look for ways to trim your budget and save a nice nest egg. You're just starting out in your life together. No doubt you have big plans that involve large purchases, from a first home to a vacation getaway, from future children to future exotic adventures, from buying another car to investing together in a start-up business venture.

There are myriad ways to save money. Here are just a few that you can do together. Help each other stick to these well-meaning plans.

Keep a coin jar. Periodically empty the change from your wallet, pockets, and purses into a communal coin jar (it can be any kind of container—a Mason jar, a piggy bank, an old can) and, when full, bring it to a bank to exchange for bills whenever the jar is full. Deposit the money in one of your joint savings accounts or use it for the monthly dinner out that you've rationed for yourselves as part of your overall budget.

Pack a homemade lunch. Prepare dinners with leftovers in mind, or buy the makings for lunch when you go grocery shopping. Stick a love note in your partner's lunch bag to make the hand-crafted sandwich even better.

Carpool. With each other or with coworkers.

Consolidate communication and cable. You can often get a discount when you buy Internet access, cell and landline service, and cable from the same provider.

Call your service companies and negotiate. You may be able to negotiate savings, such as a more favorable interest rate on a credit card or a discount on a newspaper subscription/delivery plan, just by calling and asking for it. If the company says no, threaten to cancel and sign up with a competitor. They may just come around.

Insulate and go green. To lower utility bills, block drafts around windows and doors. Agree on a thermostat sweet-spot that's relatively low—65 to 68 degrees—and bulk up by donning sweaters, electric blankets, and each other (you are newlyweds, after all). Whenever you need to replace an appliance or windows, opt for eco-friendly, efficient options that will reduce your utility bills.

Buy a water filter. Attach it to your faucet instead of buying bottled water, which quickly adds up (and whose plastic containers clog landfills).

Resolve not to splurge on lavish gifts. For birthdays, anniversaries, winter holidays, and Valentine's Day—you may decide that your gift to each other is to sock away another $50 or $100 each in your down-payment fund.

Eat at home more often. Considering that the average restaurant mark-up is 200 percent, it pays to prepare meals at home.

Dealing with Different Spending and Saving Styles

Love has nothing to do with money. You may be in love with someone whose saving and spending habits you don't love one bit. If you think that's the case, an assessment of your similarities and differences might be in order. If you took any marriage prep classes, you probably talked about your separate attitudes toward money and your financial goals. If you didn't have that talk then, you'll need to have it now.

Before sitting down to discuss, take the quiz below. If you and your partner choose different answers for the majority of the questions, that's a good sign that your financial philosophies are not in tune. After taking the quiz, review the questions and discuss why you chose the answers you did.

[**1**] What would you do if you received a surprise check for $5,000?

a) Use the money for the down payment on a house or car.

b) Deposit it in long-term savings.

c) Go to Las Vegas and try to double it.

[**2**] Finish this sentence: My parents . . .

a) taught me how to budget when I was in grade school.

b) treated shopping like a sport.

c) never talked about money.

[**3**] I hold onto clothes until . . .

a) they have holes.

b) the following season, when they're no longer in fashion.

c) I've never gotten rid of a piece of clothing.

[**4**] Right now in my wallet, there's . . .

a) some emergency cash plus my ATM and credit cards.

b) I have no idea what's in my wallet.

c) some photos of my nieces and nephews.

[**5**] How would you pay for an upcoming vacation?

a) Credit card—charge it now and pay for it later.

b) I'd trim the fat from my budget for a few months to save for the vacation.

c) I'd take money out of my savings.

[**6**] How often are you overdue paying bills?

a) I'm pretty good, but every few months I let some slide.

b) I've never paid a bill late.

c) You can count on one hand the number of times I've been late.

After talking about your answers to these questions, you have a pretty good idea whether you're both spenders, both savers, or one of each.

SPENDER VS. SAVER: What Type Are You?

SIGNS YOU MAY BE A SPENDER:

1. You use a credit card for all your purchases.
2. You are consistently late paying bills.
3. Your favorite hobby is shopping.

Take the time to determine your saving and spending habits.

SIGNS YOU MAY BE A SAVER:

1. You wear your clothes until they have holes.
2. You properly budget each month and put money aside for emergencies.
3. Your parents taught you to save for things you wanted.

If you're both spenders: You will probably have a lot of good times followed abruptly by an intensely miserable period of debt. Understand that this situation is a near certitude and devise strategies to curb your instincts—and to goad each other's impulses—to take spontaneous trips and pay large amounts for unnecessary items.

If you're both savers: It's wonderful that you're compatible and that you each know exactly how much is in the bank at any given time, but too much of a good thing can be stifling. Make sure to set aside some money for both small and occasional larger rewards. It's admirable to save for the future, but it's important to enjoy the present, too.

If one is a saver and the other is a spender: Be careful not to cast your partner's differences in a negative light, that is, don't think of your saver-partner as "cheap" and of your spender-partner as "frivolous." Instead, aim to understand what made your partner that way in the first place and work to find a happy medium.

Here are some of the major influences that mold a person's money-sense style:

■ **Economic background.** If one of you grew up in a well-to-do family whereas the other was part of a family that struggled to meet monthly bills, you will most likely have vastly different outlooks on money. Be sensitive to the other's history with money and try to formulate a healthy relationship with your finances—together.

■ **Family money-culture.** Your outlooks may differ even if you both came from identical family situations. If your parents were constantly worried about money (regardless of whether they needed to be) and constantly saved instead of spent, it's difficult not to inherit that attitude. The same goes for the opposite: If your parents were spenders, you'll probably have the same inclination and may indulge in shopping sprees as rewards or as comforting activities. Be honest about your spending habits and discuss potential problems—either your own or your partner's.

■ **Income and circumstances.** If one spouse makes more money now, and has always made more money, you might be more comfortable spending it. Give your partner some time to get used to the jump in income—habits are hard to break, and he or she might continue to feel the need to live by a strict budget for some time.

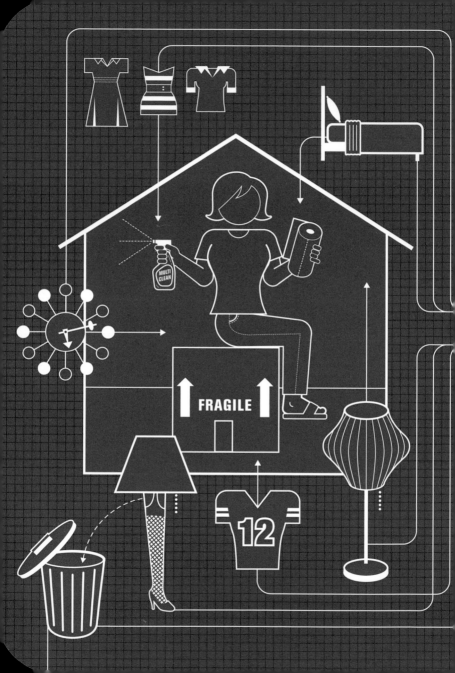

[Chapter 3]

The Nest

uLug

ONLY
$**19**$95
*PER MILE

Buying a House

This purchase is probably one of the biggest you'll make in your entire life, so it's important to think long and hard about whether you can afford to buy a house and what kind of house you'd like to buy.

How to Know When You're Ready

It was more difficult to know whether or not your spouse was the right person to marry than it will be to figure out if you're ready for homeownership. The two are in fact very different. Deciding to marry is a decision based largely on emotion. Deciding to buy a home should be the opposite: wholly detached from emotion. When you're figuring out if you're ready to be a homeowner, you need to look at your financial situation and at the local housing market with an analytical, unfeeling eye.

Here's a checklist to gauge readiness:

❑ Can you find a house you're happy with that eats up only a third of your household income?

❑ Do you have enough saved for a 20 percent down payment?

❑ Are you prepared to move and stay in the house for at least five years, preferably more? In addition to a down payment and mortgage, there are extensive closing and selling costs, and if your house isn't guaranteed to appreciate quickly, these will eat up your investment. If the real-estate market is weak, be prepared to stay in a house for ten years or more.

Common Terms

Do you know what the following words mean in the context of real estate? Not knowing them doesn't mean you're not ready, it just means you have some studying to do.

Appreciation/Depreciation: In the context of real estate, these terms apply to a home's value. You should aim to buy a house with enough overall positive qualities that it's bound to go up, not down, in value by the time you're ready to sell.

Flip/Flipper: In a strong market, home flippers buy homes, renovate them, and then turn around and immediately put them back on the market to sell them for a profit.

Oversupply: An oversupply of homes on the market means that homes are staying on the market for a long time. This indicates a buyers' market and that there's room to negotiate prices lower than the list price.

House-Poor: If you buy a house so expensive that your monthly mortgage payments preclude you from eating anything but Cup-a-Noodle and from dressing in anything but hand-me-downs, you're house-poor.

Credit Report: A report that contains detailed information about your credit history, including a record of all late payments on bills, loans, and credit cards and information on your bank accounts and spending history. Potential lenders (such as for a mortgage) look at this report and at the subsequent credit score to determine how risky it is to lend money to you.

Location, Location, Location

You've decided you're ready to own a house. How do you decide which neighborhood and which type of home? Here's what you should consider:

Location. The old maxim—"Location, location, location"—is true. This is priority number one in terms of a home's appreciation. Even if you can make do with a house that's in the flight path of a major airport or neighbors a major highway, chances are future buyers won't, and your house will languish on the market.

Neighborhood and quality of life. Does the neighborhood have an active neighborhood association? Are people upgrading their homes and investing in the area? Are there good public schools (this is also a factor in a home's appreciation) and nearby restaurants and supermarkets? If it's an urban setting, is it easy to find street parking?

Price. Figure out what you can afford each month for mortgage payments, plus how much you can put down up-front, and make sure to factor in closing costs (about 4 to 5 percent of the sale price, depending on where you live). Come up with a range in which you feel comfortable.

Size. How much house do you need? Don't decide by looking at how much house your friends have. Don't worry about keeping up with the Joneses. Stay focused on yourselves and your own needs.

Features. Write down your top three priorities as far as a home's features. Is it most important to you that the home has decent outdoor space and a great kitchen, or are you more concerned with a garage and an office? Is a big closet a must? Have you always wanted an old house or are you a fan of new construction? Writing down your priorities will help keep you focused during the house hunt.

Proximity to family. Do you want to be close to your family? How close? The ideal distance from in-laws is a 90-minute drive (close enough to visit but not so close they're likely to pop in frequently, unannounced).

Commute. Consider how you're going to commute from the house to work, since this is a major quality-of-life concern. You don't want to buy a house only to end up living in your car.

House-Hunting Tips

It's easy to be distracted by the cosmetic shortcomings of the homes you tour during a house hunt, but you should be more concerned about the structure and bones. The trick to evaluating a house is to see past these easy-to-fix elements.

Here's what you shouldn't worry about:

- Horrendous paint colors (you'll paint over it)
- Outdated wallpaper (it's easy to get rid of)
- Ugly or stained carpeting (it's easy to replace)
- The seller's furniture (it won't be there when you move in)
- Clutter (imagine what the room would look like without it)
- Ugly landscaping (you can change it)

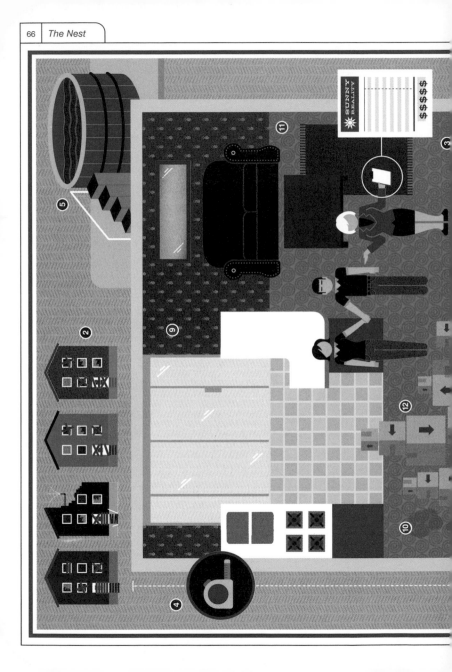

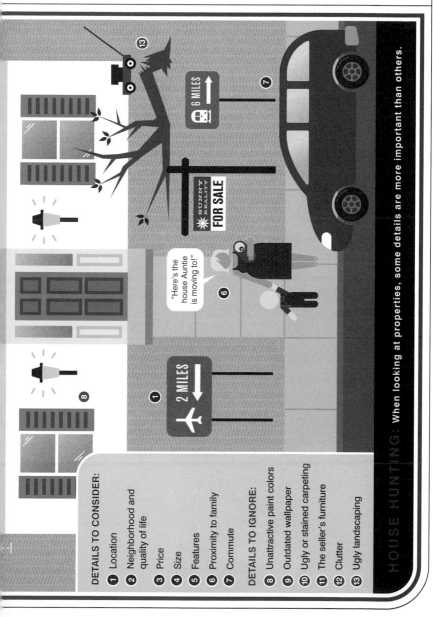

Here's what you should worry about. (These are things that are difficult to change or will cost a great deal to fix.):

- Obvious water damage
- Noise from neighbors or the street
- Lack of light
- Mouse droppings (indicates more mice and a lack of maintenance)
- Shared property with neighbors
- Bars on the windows (indicates high-crime area)
- Too-low ceilings (hard to change)
- Outdated kitchens and bathrooms (these are fixable, but not for cheap)
- A bad view (you're stuck with it forever)
- Old, drafty windows (expensive to replace)
- No room for expansion

Moving

Some newlyweds report that moving in together is an even tougher transition than saying the words "I do." This makes sense, especially if one or both newlyweds are accustomed to living alone. If you've recently had roommates, this process can be easier, since you'll be accustomed to making space for someone else and having to respect another person's space, ideas, and style.

The Mental Move

The physical move is tough, but mental preparedness is perhaps the greater hurdle. By adulthood, a person has a good idea of what he or she wants in a home. This may be a serene, uncluttered space that telegraphs the presence of a quiet, cultured soul. Or it could be more like a dorm room with band posters and a drum set in the corner. If a couple is composed of one of each—a serene person and a dorm-room person—there might be some trouble soon after move-in day. Here are some things to keep in mind:

Don't assume the other person is going to change. Chances are you already have a good idea of your spouse's decorating and living style (and vice versa) since you likely spent some time in each other's homes while you were dating. If your new partner is the dorm-room type, don't expect him to change as soon as you move in together. Rather, expect to compromise so that you both feel comfortable in your new, shared home.

If possible, move somewhere that's new to you both. If you move out of your place and into your partner's, there's a chance you'll be afforded one drawer, half a closet, and a shelf on a bookcase. It can be hard to feel at home if you constantly feel like a guest in your spouse's space. It's often better for the relationship to start fresh in a space that's new to both—in "our" space rather than in "my" space—where each has an equal say in the decor.

Heed a pronoun change. Even if the place was formerly "my" place, make sure to describe it now as "our" place. Say the words, and the behavior will follow.

Expect friction. Moving is hard. And moving into a living situation that has the word "forever" dangling above it is an extra stressor. At least with a roommate, you know the lease will eventually be up. Expect spats, but when you do disagree, defuse the situation by trying to find something humorous. Then stop and think about your partner's wonderful, positive qualities that you wouldn't want to live without.

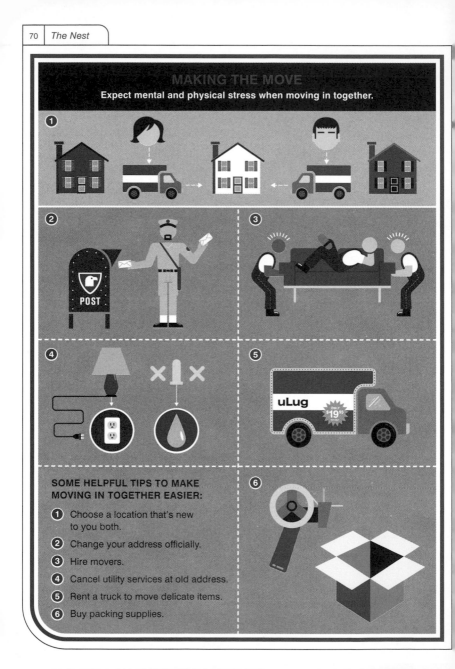

The Physical Move

The mechanics of moving are actually much easier than gauging emotional preparedness. Here are some musts for the month and weeks before the move:

Change your address officially. Contact the post office, magazines, credit cards, and the IRS. Decide how to notify everyone else of your new address—will you do it by e-mail or will you send a card through the regular mail?

Hire movers. Ask friends for referrals. Many movers are less than trustworthy and can hold your stuff hostage until you pay them a fee that's higher than their initial quote.

Cancel utility services. Or take them out of your name on the day of your move. Call the gas, electric, cable, and phone companies.

Buy packing supplies. Gather boxes (more than you think you'll need), packing tape, and markers for labeling the contents.

Decide how you're going to move yourself. You're not going to ride with the movers, so, if needed, arrange to rent or borrow a car to move yourselves, your pets, and your valuables—laptop, important papers, inherited jewels—that you don't want to entrust to the movers.

Pack. It depends on the size of your place, but at the very least start packing at least a week before the move. Tackle packing one room at a time, marking the boxes accordingly. If you're very organized, type out a list of the items that are in each box. Pack the items you'll need immediately in their own box and mark it "Essentials," so you know exactly which one it is.

Merging Stuff

Because of the trend toward marrying later in life, most newlyweds come to the marriage with a lot of stuff. Often each person already has dishes, a couch, a bed, a coffee table, armchairs, etc. How do you decide whose stuff to keep and whose to get rid of? People who subscribe to the saying "What's mine is mine and what's yours is junk" are not going to succeed in forging a healthy relationship.

Tackle the process systematically:

Map out your needs. Figure out the furniture you need in your home—for example, is your living room so big that it will easily fit two couches and four armchairs, or is it more of a one-couch, one-armchair living space? Are you moving into a three-bedroom or a one-bedroom home? How many books do you have? Are there enough built-in bookshelves in the new house to accommodate them or will you need to bring in some standalone shelving units? How many?

Take inventory. Prioritize. Now that you have an idea of what you need, take inventory of what you have. Each newlywed should make a list of his or her belongings, including appliances, furniture, art, accessories, and tableware. Place a star next to the five things you absolutely can't live without.

Combine lists. Compare your lists for overlapping items. If any are doubles of something one of you can't part with (a starred item), decide to get rid of the one that's not starred. Both parties need to be willing to make sacrifices, especially if you're moving into a small place. If you can't decide between duplicates, choose the one that's cleaner, newer, and in better condition.

Practice empathy. Although at times it may be impossible to understand your partner's dogmatic attitude toward your Led Zeppelin poster, try stepping into her shoes. Look around at her belongings—does she own anything that resembles your Zeppelin poster in style or content? Is the poster likely to blend into the home that you're planning to make your own as a couple? If the answers to these questions are "no," you might be holding on too tightly to the past. Be willing to let go in order to make room for new memories.

Purge. Haul the items to the curb or the Salvation Army, or try to sell them on Web sites such as Craigslist or Ebay if you think there's still some life left in them.

Expert Tip: Things that should definitely go include artifacts from past relationships, broken items, and outdated kitsch.

Decluttering

Merging inevitably leads to a feeling of being overwhelmed by stuff. Unless one or both of you is a total neatnik/minimalist, you're going to have twice the stuff once you move in together. And unless you move into a home that's twice the size of your former abode, that will likely be too much stuff.

Join forces as a couple and declutter. Make it as fun as possible—set a decluttering date, put on some music that fills both of you with purposeful energy, and order a pizza to eat as your reward.

Be systematic about the process:

[1] Equip yourselves with decluttering tools: at least three containers marked "Keep," "Give Away," and "Throw Away." Line the "Throw Away" container with a garbage bag.

[**2**] Declutter in small increments: Set a timer or keep an eye on the clock and work for an hour before taking a break. (The time will pass before you know it.)

[**3**] Go room by room.

[**4**] Start at the entrance of the first room and work your way around the room, clockwise.

[**5**] Work in small chunks: One drawer at a time, one corner at a time, one shelf at a time.

[**6**] Don't stop and dwell on an object. Quickly ask yourself these questions:

- Have I used it in the last year?
- Do I have another one that's better?
- Do I really need two?
- Do I really love it or does it just make me feel guilty about whoever gave it to me?
- Does it have sentimental value? If yes, how much on a scale of 1 to 10?

If the object doesn't make the cut, be ruthless and decide whether it should be thrown or given away.

[**7**] When the timer goes off, decide whether to keep going or to stop for the day. When you decide you're finished, take the "throw away" bag and put it in a trash can. Take the "give away" box and stow it in your car so that the next time you're out, you can drive by the thrift shop and drop it off. Find a place immediately for everything in your "keep" box. You may just find that you reconsider some of these items as you're putting them away.

Man Rooms

This is a space whose existence may have sprung from the recent trend toward bigger houses and later marriages, which often result in men having ample time to amass more stuff that their spouses may not want in the house. More so than women, men tend to hold on to items that (a) remind them of high school and/or college; (b) are associated with their favorite sports teams; and (c) have seen better days. The man room is the solution to the problem that inevitably arises when a man moves in with a woman and the woman says, "You need to get rid of that ratty couch, that neon beer sign, and that collection of giant Styrofoam fingers, *or else*."

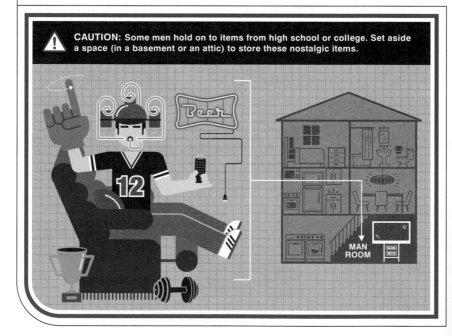

CAUTION: Some men hold on to items from high school or college. Set aside a space (in a basement or an attic) to store these nostalgic items.

Man rooms are commonly found in the following places. (Note that these all tend to have a common hidden-away, doghouse vibe.)

- The basement
- The garage
- An outbuilding or shed
- The attic
- An office space far from the home's most frequented rooms

If you don't have space for a man room, at least make sure you're moving into a space that allows for each partner to have his or her domain, i.e., a private nook to escape to when alone time is needed.

Decorating

Beware the newlyweds who claim that one partner is making all the decor decisions because the other "doesn't care." This is never true, and even if both partners subscribe to this myth, the truth will bubble over and erupt either explosively or slowly, in a passive-aggressive drip. The fact is that both people are living in the home, so both should feel comfortable and happily surrounded by things they cherish.

Blending Styles

You already have a good idea of each other's styles. Now comes the task of blending them. Here are some ways to do so without too much difficulty.

Divvy up the rooms. If your styles are really so different that they'll never find common ground, split up the spaces evenly. He gets his man room. She gets the living room. He gets the kitchen. She gets an office.

Make an inspiration folder. Go through a stack of magazines and tear out pictures of rooms that appeal to each of you. Then find the ones you both can agree on. Store these in a folder as inspiration to keep in mind when you're out looking for furniture or shopping for paint colors.

Balance between masculine and feminine. Don't go too far in either direction to demonstrate how great you are at compromising. A house full of leather club chairs and paintings of dogs playing poker isn't going to make anyone happy for very long. Neither will a home that's a study in shabby chic—all white, distressed French-country furniture and frilly window treatments. Find a happy medium.

Decorating on a Dime

Newlyweds usually don't have much disposable income, so the decorating needs to be done on the cheap and, often, gradually, as couples save enough money to spend on each room. No need to buy everything at once—spread the enjoyment over the years so that you're not so broke you can't go out and celebrate occasionally.

Decorating Time Line

Take it slowly. When you move into your new house, put your heads together to come up with a master plan for tackling each project/room. This will keep you focused as you make your way systematically through the house or apartment. Your master plan might look something like this:

[1] **March:** Buy headboard and low dresser to share in bedroom.

[2] **April:** Get window treatments for kitchen (for privacy—windows are right on the street) and in the bedroom to keep out morning sunlight.

[3] **May:** Living room. Wait till move-in date to ascertain what is needed.

[4] **May/June:** Buy BBQ and outdoor table and chairs for backyard.

[5] **Next Fall:** Start to think about kitchen redo.

Cheap Tricks

Professional decorators employ plenty of strategies to make a room look expensively done even if they were limited to a shoestring budget. Here are some of their tricks:

Check online classifieds and auction sites. Craigslist and Ebay are full of other people's trash that could be your treasure. Local Craigslist listings are the most economical because you can pick up the items instead of having to pay for shipping.

Brush up on DIY techniques. Knowing how to refinish and paint a dresser or how to reline a lampshade and rewire an old light fixture will make your trips to the flea markets and thrift shops that much more successful.

Welcome hand-me-downs. Your parents, your friends' parents, and maybe even your friends might have pieces they're not using that are collecting dust in their basement or in storage. Ask around.

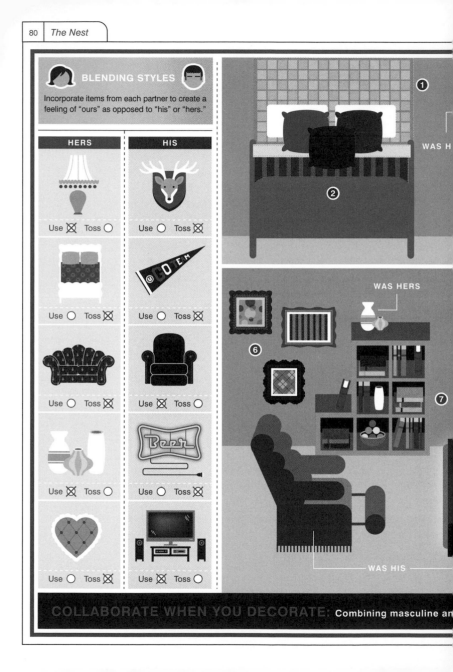

BLENDING STYLES

Incorporate items from each partner to create a feeling of "ours" as opposed to "his" or "hers."

HERS	HIS
Use ☒ Toss ○	Use ○ Toss ☒
Use ○ Toss ☒	Use ○ Toss ☒
Use ○ Toss ☒	Use ☒ Toss ○
Use ☒ Toss ○	Use ○ Toss ☒
Use ○ Toss ☒	Use ☒ Toss ○

① ② ⑥ ⑦

WAS H

WAS HERS

WAS HIS

COLLABORATE WHEN YOU DECORATE: Combining masculine an

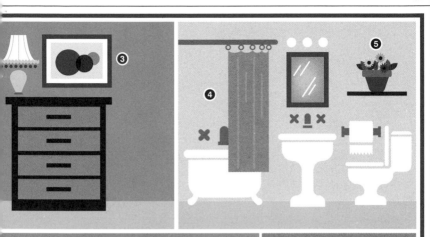

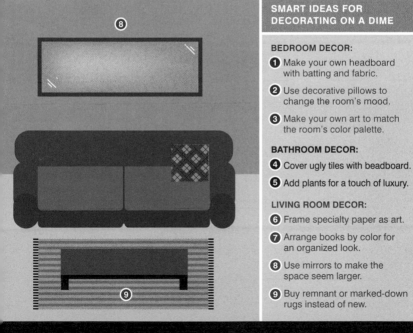

SMART IDEAS FOR DECORATING ON A DIME

BEDROOM DECOR:

1. Make your own headboard with batting and fabric.

2. Use decorative pillows to change the room's mood.

3. Make your own art to match the room's color palette.

BATHROOM DECOR:

4. Cover ugly tiles with beadboard.

5. Add plants for a touch of luxury.

LIVING ROOM DECOR:

6. Frame specialty paper as art.

7. Arrange books by color for an organized look.

8. Use mirrors to make the space seem larger.

9. Buy remnant or marked-down rugs instead of new.

minine elements will create a balanced home where you both feel comfortable.

Thrift stores and flea markets. Again, other people's junk or near-junk can be your treasure.

Paint. Painting a room is the cheapest way to make the biggest impact. Pick a color that's stimulating if it's for the living room or office; serene if it's for the bedroom; and cheerful if it's for the kitchen. If you're dying to experiment with fuchsia, do a patch test first: Paint a small section of the wall fuchsia and see if you still like it after a few days. Notice how the hue changes as the light changes in the room.

Know when to skimp. Spend the money for a nice mattress, couch, and office chair, since these are the items that directly affect your comfort and your health. (If you're not sitting and sleeping correctly, you'll end up spending money on physical therapy and massages.) It's not as essential if your dresser is made of wood veneer instead of solid wood as it is if your couch is lumpy or too stiff.

Cheap Decorating in the Living Room

Mirrors. Mirrors really do make a room look larger, and they are available in a range of price points. It's much more tasteful to make use of mirrors in a living room than in a bedroom, where too many can emit a sleazy vibe.

Books. Decorate with your favorite volumes. Stack them on the floor for an impromptu occasional table. Arrange them by color on the bookshelf. Use them on an end table as a plant pedestal.

Cheap art. Find inexpensive frames at a discount store and buy a group of four or six identical ones. Frame beautiful pieces of scrapbook or other specialty paper and hang them in a group for an instant and inexpensive but lovely look. Other things to frame in a group are record or CD covers;

magazine covers; pieces of fabric; wallpaper; and photos from your vacations. Make sure the mats and frames are identical for a finished feel.

Remnants. Many stores that sell rugs and carpeting also offer a supply of remnants and possibly a collection of marked-down floor coverings, too.

Cheap Decorating in the Bedroom
Headboard. Create the illusion of a headboard by hanging a collection of art in a pyramid over your bed. Another option: Hang a piece of fabric the width of your bed on the wall behind it. You can also make a headboard yourself by covering a piece of wood with batting and fabric.

Art. Visit an art-supply store for blank canvas and some decorative stencils—or letter or image stencils if you'd rather create a realistic piece. Also pick up a few pencils, paint colors, and brushes and get to work creating your own masterpiece that matches your bedroom's palette.

Decorative pillows. Change the throw pillows on your bed now and then to change the room's mood.

Cheap Decorating in the Bathroom
Cover ugly tiles. If the tiles on your bathroom walls are dated, try buying sheets of beadboard at a large hardware or home-goods store. It's usually white but you can paint it any color. Attach it to your walls with liquid glue, and voilà! The tiles vanish instantly. Another way to dress up ugly tiles is to find tile decals either to cover them or to devise a more interesting or pleasant pattern.

Plants. An unexpected spot of green in the bathroom will make it feel luxurious, like a hotel or spa bathroom.

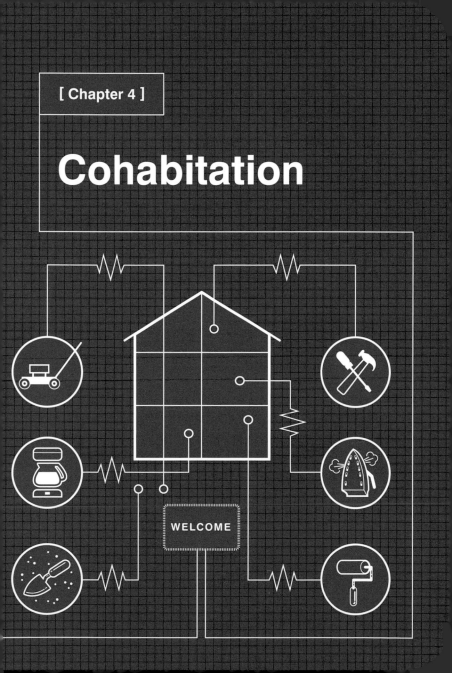

[Chapter 4]

Cohabitation

WELCOME

There are positive and negative ways to view your new roommate/partner-in-life. Is he or she an annoyance who cuts into your me-time and hogs the remote control? Or is he or she your new around-the-clock playtime person who's always there to celebrate life's joys and commiserate over the inevitable bummers? The answer is: both. Sometimes you'll be thrilled to realize your spouse is waiting for you at home. Other times, you might wish you were returning to an empty house. The balance depends on learning to live with another's habits and to give each other space. To build a home life where each person is happy, play to each person's strengths and quirks. Don't try to make your spouse into something he or she is not.

House Rules

After the honeymoon comes the routine. Once the novelty of being newlyweds wears off, the day-to-day reality of living together can risk becoming mundane. It can also become annoying. There is the good and the bad, but you can take control of the environment to turn the situation toward the good, most of the time. Here are some tips for doing so.

Establish house rules. These will evolve as you get used to living together and as you become accustomed to the other's habits. The rules might be, "We only talk about bills every other Wednesday" or "No going to bed angry."

Treat each other as you would treat a roommate. Show the same respect for your partner's opinions and space. Just because he's "yours," doesn't mean you can abuse him. (We often treat our loved ones worse than we do our acquaintances, so don't fall into that trap.)

Seek solutions. Maybe you're the type of person who reads the Sunday newspaper in one fell swoop and pops it into the recycling bin by noon that day. He spreads it out over the week—and all over the living room, kitchen, and bedroom. Don't let it drive you crazy. Instead, invest in an attractive basket and ask him to store it there while he's making his way through the news.

Remember, neither of you is a mind-reader. There is no "right" way. Your new spouse has no way of knowing, for example, that the "right" way to store leftovers is in plastic containers, not in your nice dishes; that you don't run the dishwasher until it's full; that you never put the wood-handled knives in the dishwasher. Cut each other some slack. And instead of imposing your own way, come up with new ideas for doing things and tackling tasks, together.

Choose your battles. Is it really going to do anyone any good to yell every time your partner forgets to put down the toilet seat? Don't sweat the small stuff.

Routines

Routines are essential to a happy living environment. They stave off chaos and bring comfort to one and all.

The Morning Routine

If one of you is a morning person, then that person should get up first, start the coffee, and pick up the newspaper. This is your time of the day to be the better partner. If neither of you are morning people, lean on each other to make it out the door in time for work. Divvy up the morn-

ing chores—one makes coffee and breakfast; the other packs bagged lunches, etc.

The After-Work Routine

We all have different methods of decompressing after a long day. You may need to sit in silence for a half hour when you get home from work. Your partner may prefer chatting instantly about everything that happened that day. Learn each other's decompression styles and act accordingly. This could lead to the formation of a house rule: No talking about our days until the last one in the door has been home for twenty minutes.

Different Decompressing Styles

Chatty Cathy: Spilling over with news about the day, items of interest learned, and questions about next weekend's plans. People who work alone and from home are often this style, since they've had little social interaction during the day.

Silent Steve: Needs a buffer period between work and home, whether it's the result of a long day at work or not. This person wants to walk in the door, change into comfortable clothes, and pour a drink before beginning to parse the day's events.

Meditative Molly: This type needs even more intense decompression time while transitioning from the workday into the evening. He or she may need to sit alone in a quiet room with her eyes closed for a few minutes, especially if her workday was particularly long and harrowing.

The Evening and Weekend Routine

You're going to spend almost every night for the rest of your lives together ("almost," because one of you might be traveling some of these nights). Don't make the mistake of spending each night and most of the weekend sitting on the couch, watching TV. Your relationship will slowly turn into a boring, indefinable blob rather than an expression of two very interesting individuals who've banded together. Throw in some off-the-cuff rituals. Your relationship and your mental health will benefit from the lack of the mundane. Some ideas:

■ **Game night.** Play cards, Scrabble, or some other game. You could even play video games, although it's nice not to be staring at a screen, since most people do this all day.

■ **Happy hour.** Pick a night once every few weeks to mix cocktails and sit outside or on your deck and enjoy each other's company.

■ **Entertain.** Enjoy other people's company as well as each other's. Have friends over for dinner regularly or invite them to join in on game night.

■ **Exercise.** Engage in a fun cardiovascular activity together, such as bike riding, gardening, tennis, hiking, or miniature golf.

■ **Cuddle on the couch**. Record the TV shows you don't want to miss during the week and watch them together—without commercials—one or two nights or over the weekend.

■ **Flashback.** Don't forget the fun things you did when you were single. Travel together. Take a wine-tasting or art class together. Learn to cook. Go to a museum. Volunteer. These activities are just as much fun when you are part of a couple as they were when you were single.

GETTING INTO THE SWING OF THINGS: A consistent routine is

MORNING ROUTINE

THE MORNING ROUTINE
If you are a morning person, help your spouse by:

1. Picking up the newspaper
2. Making the coffee

THE AFTER-WORK ROUTINE
Learn each other's decompression style and act accordingly.

3. SILENT STEVE: Needs a quiet buffer period between work and home.
4. CHATTY CATHY: Spilling over with conversation, possibly due to a lack of social interaction during the day.
5. MEDITATIVE MOLLY: Needs intense decompression time.

EVENING AND WEEKEND ROUTINES
Prevent your relationship from becoming boring with activities such as:

6. Game night
7. Inviting friends over for cocktails
8. Exercise

AFTER-WORK ROUTINE

EVENING AND WEEKEND ROUTINES

DIVIDING CHORES

One of the aspects of living together that you need to figure out right away is division of labor. Who's going to do what and how often? Nail down this detail at the start so there are no false expectations, which always lead to hurt feelings. List the chores that need to be done and then mark your name next to the ones you don't mind doing. If there are one or two that you absolutely detest, voice that, too. Once you've figured out likes and dislikes (within reason—no one really likes to do chores), dole them out evenly.

Here are some sample lists of household chores:

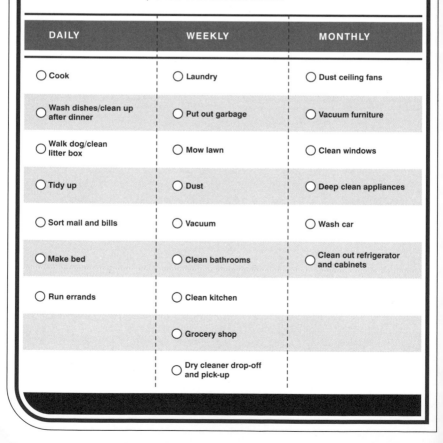

DAILY	WEEKLY	MONTHLY
○ Cook	○ Laundry	○ Dust ceiling fans
○ Wash dishes/clean up after dinner	○ Put out garbage	○ Vacuum furniture
○ Walk dog/clean litter box	○ Mow lawn	○ Clean windows
○ Tidy up	○ Dust	○ Deep clean appliances
○ Sort mail and bills	○ Vacuum	○ Wash car
○ Make bed	○ Clean bathrooms	○ Clean out refrigerator and cabinets
○ Run errands	○ Clean kitchen	
	○ Grocery shop	
	○ Dry cleaner drop-off and pick-up	

Laundry

Men who are thrown into doing laundry that includes women's under-things are easily intimidated. Until now, their whole perspective on bras was limited to figuring out how to undo them. Plus, this activity has a high learning curve. Women have been washing their bras since they were teenagers, and they had their moms to mentor them. Who's going to pass along the same information to hapless husbands? On the other hand, women might not be that familiar with how men clean their suits and button-down work shirts. Here's a step-by-step cheat sheet:

How to wash a bra

[1] Attach any clasps so that they don't catch on anything.

[2] Put the bra in a lingerie bag (usually a mesh fabric zip-up bag) that further prevents it from snagging or getting snagged. If you don't have a lingerie bag, use a pillowcase and knot it on top.

[3] Wash on a gentle cycle in cold or warm water (i.e., not hot).

[4] Wash with like colors and items that are similarly light and delicate (i.e., T-shirts, other bras, underwear, pajamas). Do not wash with towels or jeans.

[5] When you take the bra out of the wash, reshape the cups.

[6] Air-dry the bra on a clothesline or drying rack, preferably flat so that the straps don't stretch.

[7] If you must put the bra in a dryer, use the lowest setting.

How to wash other delicates (pantyhose, slips, lace undergarments)

[**1**] Follow steps 1 through 4 on the previous page.

[**2**] When you remove the delicates from the washer, lay them on a towel and roll it up to remove excess water. Repeat if necessary.

[**3**] Dry flat on a rack or hang.

How to wash button-down shirts

[**1**] Check and empty the pockets.

[**2**] Remove stays from the collar.

[**3**] Read the special care instructions to make sure the item is not dry-clean only. If not, follow the instructions on the label.

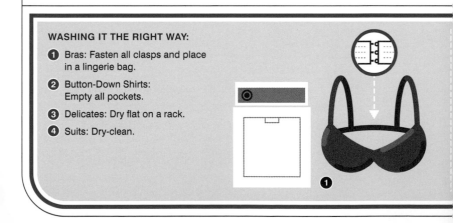

WASHING IT THE RIGHT WAY:

❶ Bras: Fasten all clasps and place in a lingerie bag.

❷ Button-Down Shirts: Empty all pockets.

❸ Delicates: Dry flat on a rack.

❹ Suits: Dry-clean.

How to wash suits

Suits (both men's and women's) are no different than other clothes that need to be dry-cleaned. Do not dry-clean them more than necessary, because frequent dry-cleaning lowers the shelf-life of any garment. With a man's suit, over-cleaning tends to make the fabric shiny.

How to wash dirty, sweaty sports uniforms

[1] Buy a pair of tongs especially for this task.

[2] Wash these items on their own—no need to sully other garments.

[3] Use hot water.

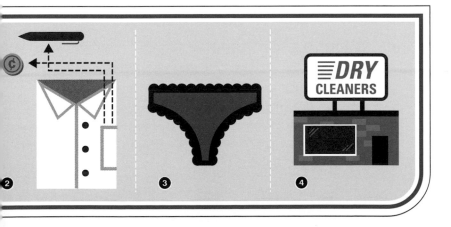

Cooking and Eating

Ozzie and Harriet, the Cleavers, and other 1950s TV husbands and wives set the tone for a clear gender divide that places the female partner in the kitchen and the male partner in the living room, with feet up and smoking a pipe. Though that was a long time ago, this paradigm has been hard for society to shake. Many people still have certain expectations when entering marriage, and if you both favor this type of arrangement, then all is well.

But if not, then it's important to quash this expectation before the female partner becomes bitter about having to cook dinner every night, and the male partner turns into a nightmarish retro version of himself. The way to do so is to communicate about the kitchen and who does what. Couples today are more complicated—both of you probably have jobs and one of you is probably a natural cook. A household composed of two busy partners, neither of whom is in charge of the dinner schedule, can easily slip into either chaos or a nightly pizza routine. The latter is probably why most newlyweds gain an average of twenty-five pounds during their first five years of marriage.

Establish a Dinner Routine/Plan

Dinner makes up the bulk of the quality time you'll spend together during the workweek. Plan ahead so that you're not wasting it staring at each other and asking, "What are we doing for dinner?" Having a plan will make you feel organized and as though you're working together as a team, mastering this new life as husband and wife, as opposed to just staying one step ahead of the game. Talk to each other to come up with a weekly plan that you can carry into the months ahead. The components of this plan include:

- Going out to dinner (who makes reservations?)
- Staying in for dinner (who cooks? who cleans?)
- Staying in for dinner and ordering takeout
- Staying in for dinner and eating leftovers
- Wild card (an unplanned night that should probably happen over the weekend)

There are five components that you need to fit into a seven-day schedule. Decide what works for you based on your budget—if you're trying to save money, go easy on eating out. Here's a sample weekly plan:

- **Monday:** Homemade meal (wife)
- **Tuesday:** Leftovers from Monday
- **Wednesday:** Takeout
- **Thursday:** Pasta night (husband)
- **Friday:** Eat out
- **Saturday:** Wild card
- **Sunday:** Homemade meal (prepared together)

Grocery Shopping

Decide where grocery shopping fits into your weekly plan. Then add it into the routine. Having a set grocery-shopping "date" will prevent you from getting into little fights about whose turn it is to grocery shop and why the refrigerator is empty again and how come you never have any dinner plans. . . (These are common newlywed spats.)

Buy in bulk. Shop at club warehouses or buy two or more of everything at the grocery store. Food disappears more quickly than you think, especially when there are two people instead of one. And in the end, buying extra is less expensive. You'll also save time because you'll avoid multiple trips to the supermarket.

Schedule one big trip. For the sample weekly dinner schedule on the previous page, schedule a weekly shopping trip together on Sunday afternoon. Whatever you buy for the homemade dinners on Monday and Thursday will be fresh when it's time to cook.

Supplement the weekly shopping trip with smaller food-gathering jaunts:

■ Locate the nearest produce market and visit it a few times a week to incorporate fresh fruit and vegetables into your meals.

■ Visit a gourmet food shop for a little luxury to spice up the routine: a bottle of quality balsamic vinegar or an aged parmeggiano cheese, for example.

■ Find the best wine shop near your home or workplace and visit it occasionally for a nice bottle to share over pasta or takeout.

■ A bakery or bread shop provides another means of adding some excitement to the weekly regimen. Surprise your spouse with a fresh loaf of bread or delicious pastries for Sunday breakfast in bed.

STOCKING YOUR PANTRY

Every well-dressed pantry has enough staples to support the makings of a basic group of foods, from chocolate-chip cookies to pancakes to tomato sauce. Having these items on hand will allow you some spontaneity in the kitchen and will provide backup in case you have unexpected guests or your favorite takeout place suddenly shutters its doors. Here are the essentials:

DRY GOODS

- ◯ Selection of pasta
  angel hair, macaroni, penne
- ◯ Fast-cooking rice
- ◯ Couscous
- ◯ Assortment of beans
- ◯ Baking powder
- ◯ Baking soda
- ◯ Flour
  all-purpose or whole wheat
- ◯ Bisquick
- ◯ Granulated sugar
- ◯ Brown sugar
- ◯ Salt
- ◯ Dried breadcrumbs
- ◯ Nuts
- ◯ Semisweet chocolate chips

CANNED AND BOTTLED GOODS

- ◯ Can of whole tomatoes
- ◯ Olives
- ◯ Assorted soups
- ◯ Canned tuna
- ◯ Peanut butter
- ◯ Whole kernel corn
- ◯ Soy sauce
- ◯ Chicken broth
- ◯ Salsa
- ◯ Maple syrup
- ◯ Honey
- ◯ Vanilla

OILS AND VINEGARS

- ◯ Sesame oil
- ◯ Balsamic vinegar
- ◯ Red wine vinegar
- ◯ White distilled vinegar
- ◯ Cider vinegar
- ◯ Olive oil
- ◯ Cooking spray
- ◯ Cooking wine

DRIED HERBS AND SPICES

- ◯ Peppercorns (and mill)
- ◯ Sea salt or kosher salt
- ◯ Basil
- ◯ Oregano
- ◯ Tarragon
- ◯ Rosemary
- ◯ Dill weed
- ◯ Garlic powder
- ◯ Onion powder
- ◯ Cinnamon
- ◯ Ground nutmeg
- ◯ Mustard seed
- ◯ Fennel seeds

WHEN TO THROW THINGS AWAY

- Dried herbs and spices lose their flavor after six months.
- Baking soda goes flat six months after opening.
- Flour loses its effectiveness six months after opening.
- Check the sell-by date and keep the item around only a day or two after that date.

WELL-STOCKED: Keeping your cabinets and refrigerator well stocke

FREEZER:

① Frozen items (pizza, ice cream, meats)

FRIDGE:

② Top shelf: Tall items (milk, juice, dressings, wine, etc.)

③ Short shelf: Shorter items (soda cans, yogurt, etc.) and items too large or awkward for drawers

④ Fridge door: Butter, eggs, condiments, and more tall/bottled items

⑤ Drawers/crispers: Meat, fish, and cheese in one drawer; vegetables and fruits in the crisper

nd organized will make cooking at home easier.

CABINETS/PANTRY:

6 Group similar products together.

7 Keep items you use frequently on easy-to-reach shelves.

8 Store bulk items and items you use less frequently on bottom shelves.

Habits and Quirks

Your spouse inevitably has funny little habits that you used to find adorable during the honeymoon period of your dating days. Now that you're cohabitating, they are only adorable *sometimes*. Most of the time, they're a little annoying.

I Love You, but I Don't Love Your Noises

Men and women are human beings and, therefore, have the same bodily functions and general internal systems. Still, they appear to emit different sounds and at frequencies that vary wildly according to gender. If a woman did not grow up with a brother and has never had a male roommate, and if a man has never lived among women, each may be shocked, at first, by the differences that become clear soon after a couple begins living together.

These differences necessitate the establishment of more house rules that you may or may not choose to enforce, depending on your tolerance level for a person's inherent noises. Here are examples of some rules you might want to introduce into the living arrangement:

[1] No bodily noises at the table, especially while a meal is being enjoyed.

[2] This absolutely includes the "silent" varieties of such noises, i.e., SBDs and noiseless burps.

[3] If a person must pass gas, he or she must go into a different room, preferably the bathroom.

[4] If snoring occurs and is sustained longer than five minutes, the snoring partner must accept a nudge from the other partner, at which point he or she must roll over into a nonsnoring position.

[5] If a person's lip-smacking and other eating noises are loud enough to be heard over the radio when it's playing at a high volume, that person has to make an effort to turn down his or her personal volume.

In Bed

Although you may have shared a bed before you were married, sharing one post-marriage eventually becomes less about romance and more about sleep. Sleep is vitally important. If you're not getting enough, the rest of your life suffers—you do not work as efficiently; you become short-tempered; you may become easily distracted while driving and a klutz, in general. How do you adapt to having another person in your bed while ensuring that you both get enough sleep?

Get a bigger bed. There are certain scenarios that demand a king-size or California-king-size bed. These include if one of you has Restless Leg Syndrome or is an active sleeper; you have an 80-pound dog who does not want to sleep anywhere else but on the bed; one of you gets up frequently during the night. If you sleep on a bigger bed, you're less likely to experience the other person's nocturnal vibrations and jostlings.

Consider separate beds. Not like Ricky and Lucy, and not every night, but some couples do find separate sleeping arrangements to be useful one or two nights a week. If you have a guestroom and one of you is particularly restless or has a horrible cold that is keeping both of you awake, don't be embarrassed or ashamed to occasionally sleep in separate rooms for the sake of your health and well-being.

Try different mattresses. Memory-foam beds jostle much less than regular mattresses. There are also sleep-number beds, in which each partner can set a personal firmness level.

In the Bathroom

Partners are often mystified by each other's bathroom habits, and it's up to you how much you really want to know. Some newlyweds prefer being kept in the dark. Others like to share everything. Regardless, here are some hints regarding what your partner is doing in the bathroom for such a long time.

What she's doing in there

■ Tweezing/shaving/bleaching/applying delipatories/waxing unwanted facial hair and/or hair in other places
■ Drying her hair
■ Coloring her hair
■ Curling her hair
■ Straightening her hair
■ Styling her hair
■ Putting on makeup
■ Luxuriating in the tub
■ Showering—includes various latherings, shampooing, and conditioning, plus possible intensive mask applications
■ Cleansing (face)

- Toning
- Moisturizing
- Extracting blemishes
- Striking poses in front of the mirror
- Looking for cellulite/weighing herself
- Flossing/gargling/freshening her breath
- Brushing her teeth

What he's doing in there

- Number 2
- Lighting a match
- Shaving
- Clipping his toenails (be glad he's doing this in the bathroom and not on your nice living-room couch)
- Brushing his teeth
- Flossing/gargling/freshening his breath
- Checking his hairline

Note: Most couples find that a little mystery goes a long way when it comes to bodily functions and grooming habits. Yes, you know he trims his nose hairs, but you'd rather not witness it. And yes, you know she dissects her pores in the mirror every evening before bed, but it's best if she does so in privacy. Nothing kills romance more than watching your spouse groom. Everyone needs some alone time in the bathroom, and you can let your imagination run wild thinking that your spouse is doing something much sexier than removing unwanted body hair.

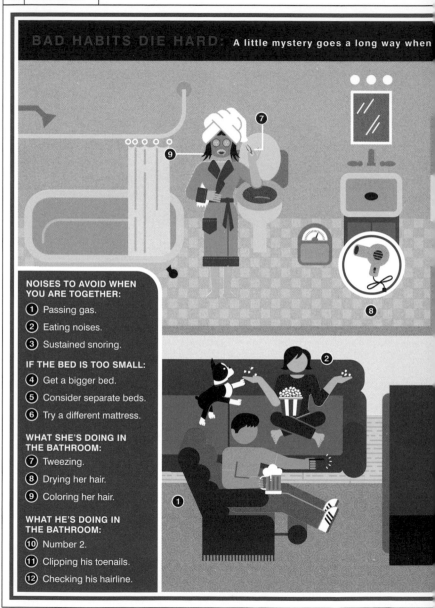

BAD HABITS DIE HARD: A little mystery goes a long way when

NOISES TO AVOID WHEN YOU ARE TOGETHER:

1. Passing gas.
2. Eating noises.
3. Sustained snoring.

IF THE BED IS TOO SMALL:

4. Get a bigger bed.
5. Consider separate beds.
6. Try a different mattress.

WHAT SHE'S DOING IN THE BATHROOM:

7. Tweezing.
8. Drying her hair.
9. Coloring her hair.

WHAT HE'S DOING IN THE BATHROOM:

10. Number 2.
11. Clipping his toenails.
12. Checking his hairline.

it comes to bodily functions and grooming habits.

In the TV Room

Most newlyweds live in a place that's big enough for only one television. How do you go about sharing when one of you loves home-design reality shows and the other is a diehard fan of the Military History channel? Or when one of you likes to watch HBO but the other prefers to play video games? A few tips:

Watch shows/films on your computer. If you really both have to be watching TV at the same time, consider buying earphones for a computer. It's easy to watch a TV show online, either by downloading the episode or by going to the show's Web site, where old episodes are posted.

Figure out a place for a small TV. Purchase a second, small set and make a place for it in the bedroom or office.

Go to a friend's house. If you and a friend are both addicted to a particular show but your spouse wants nothing to do with it, turn it into a social occasion—a weekly visit to your friend's house to hang out and watch the show. This gives your partner some alone time at home.

DVR. If both of your shows are on at the same time, tape one of them and watch it after your spouse's show.

Compromise. This is something that you're probably doing a lot of now that you're married. Try it out when it comes to sharing the TV. If both your shows are on at the same time, alternate weeks watching each other's show. Who knows? You might be surprised to find out you actually like *American Chopper* or *Dancing with the Stars*. At the very least, you'll learn a little more about your spouse's interests.

Are you a football/baseball/basketball/hockey widow(er)? During sports season, you may have more alone time and less TV time than you ever wanted. How will you cope during these months when you're missing your spouse, and your TV room has become super-fan central?

Encourage the sports fan to leave the house. Can he or she go and watch every other game at a friend's house? Plant the seed in a supportive way, and it will grow.

Plan your own activities around the games. On game nights, venture out solo to dinner and a movie with a friend. Keep yourself busy.

Strike a deal. Tell your sports fan that you'd like to arrange a deal in which, for every two hours spent watching sports, you get an hour to do something together (and the activity is of your choosing).

Chapter 5

Trust and Communication

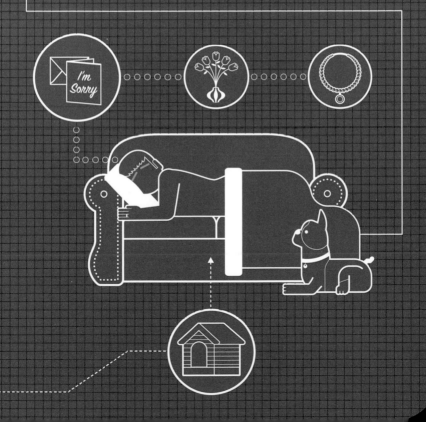

There may be as many metaphors and similes for marriage and for new marriage as there are actual marriages. Here are just a few:

■ Marriage is like a 401k: The more you invest in it, the more valuable it becomes.
■ New marriage is like a newly planted garden: It needs careful tending and feeding in order to flourish.
■ New marriage is like fire: When the flame dies down, you can stoke it or you can let it go to ash.

People have also been known to compare marriage to a roller-coaster ride, beef stew, and a snowball—the list is endless, but the messages embedded in each are the same: 1. Marriage is tough and it requires work; 2. On top of that, marriage is especially tough at the very beginning, when the blush is just beginning to fade from the rose.

So how do you start the hard work?

Self-Assessment

There's an entire psychological field populated by researchers who apply scientific method to the prediction of marital success. They've found that they can accurately assess a relationship's health—and therefore the future health of the marriage—by observing newlyweds' extraverbal and oral cues. Use their findings to take the pulse of your own foundling union.

IDENTIFY YOUR COUPLE STYLE

The first stage of self-assessment is to identify the couple style that best describes you and your spouse. Here are just a few:

COUPLE STYLE #1

The Shmoopies ♥

Hallmarks: You're very lovey-dovey with each other. You never let go of each other's hand. When you sit down, you're often sitting thigh to thigh. You frequently display a behavioral tic in which you finish each other's sentences, giggle, and then look deep into each other's eyes like a pair of lovesick teenagers. You're never apart except when you absolutely need to be.

Pros: Romance.

Cons: You risk losing yourself when you become so invested in morphing into one being. You also risk losing the friends who knew you before you met your spouse. Your relationship may quickly become boring if neither of you has individual interests and experiences to bring to the mutual table.

Problem: You have no friends left.

Solution: Your public displays of affection might be making people uncomfortable. Detach yourselves from each other when you're in the presence of others.

Problem: People nearby keep vomiting.

Solution: See Solution 1.

Problem: You have nothing to talk about.

Solution: Resolve to do something on your own or with friends at least once a week.

COUPLE STYLE #2

The Cleavers

Hallmarks: You're as 1950s as meat and potatoes, poodle skirts, and pointy bras. You observe a gender divide that's clearly in line with that of June and Ward: He wins the bread. She toasts it, uses the leftovers to make French toast, cleans up afterward, and will eventually rear the kids. As far as communication patterns go, he talks and she listens.

Pros: Nothing is left to chance. You know exactly where you stand.

Cons: This formation places the female at the weaker end of the power dynamic. She may grow tired of that status, for example, upon realizing that she has no control over her life if she has no control over the finances. This situation can lead to resentment.

Problem: The housewife gets radical and decides she wants more control.

Solution: Observe the more progressive couples around you and follow their lead.

Problem: She doesn't know how to cook.

Solution: He might not, either. Take a cooking class together.

Problem: He feels more like a parent than a husband.

Solution: See Solution #1

COUPLE STYLE #3

The Independents

Hallmarks: You may as well be roommates for the amount of time you see each other. Each of you is so deeply involved in your own career, friends, and/or outside interests that your couple time is limited to a half-asleep midnight grunt and a brief catch-up conversation in the morning as you're rushing to get ready for work.

Pros: You have a clear sense of who you are and don't rely on your spouse to complete you.

Cons: If you prioritize individuality over togetherness, you run the risk of your relationship becoming more friend-like than spouse-like. You need to figure out how to balance individuality with the needs of your relationship.

Problem: You realize you know more about your "work-husband" or "work-wife" than you do about your actual spouse.

Solution: Discuss the problem together and decide to spend less time at work and more time at home.

Problem: You're beginning to feel more like friends than like husband and wife.

Solution: Again, get out your calendars and schedule some date nights, even if it's at home for dinner and a movie. Spend time thinking up romantic gestures to let your spouse know you care.

COUPLE STYLE #4

The Pavarottis

Hallmarks: You're hardly ever "doing just fine." Instead, you're either throwing heavy objects at each other as your fights crescendo to operatic levels, or you're more deeply in love than ever. You each value the expression of emotion above all and feel that everything should always be out in the open and that repressing problems will only lead to an inauthentic relationship.

Pros: You've realized that there's a value in keeping lines of communication open. You're not afraid to show your feelings.

Cons: Becoming too caught up in drama may lead to escalating power struggles that result in you losing sight of the relationship's foundation. You may become so used to fighting, that fighting becomes the habit rather than the exception.

Problem: You're exhausted from fighting.

Solution: Resolve to pick your battles. Each time you want to fight, stop and ask yourself if it's worth it.

Problem: You like opera.

Solution: There are other, equally satisfying forms of entertainment. Try a pleasingly even-keeled sitcom or a puppet show.

Problem: You're addicted to drama.

Solution: Stop to consider the stress that's caused by all the drama. Imagine your life without the stress, and then make that vision a reality.

Self-Observation: Measuring Your "We-ness"

Now that you know your couple style, you'll be able to dig a little deeper in your self-assessment. Try to observe the following behaviors when you're together:

■ When sitting together on a couch, are you close? When choosing chairs, do you choose ones that are next to each other? If the answer is yes, do you scoot the chairs even more closely together?

[The interpretation: Sitting closely is an indicator of general physical closeness, which is a good thing in newlyweds.]

■ Do you make frequent eye contact with your spouse?

[The interpretation: Eye contact correlates positively with relationship success.]

■ When you're asked to tell the story of how you met, is there a positive or a negative cast? Do you express pride, fondness, and affection for each other, or do you express criticism?

[The interpretation: A positive image of the marriage indicates a positive perspective on the relationship.]

■ In that story of how you met, do each of you seem clear on what first attracted you to the other person?

[The interpretation: Vagueness in this regard indicates trouble.]

■ Do you express we-ness when you're talking about yourselves and your marriage, or is it all "I, I, I"?

[The interpretation: The degree to which you indicate unity in conversation belies unity or lack thereof in your marriage.]

You should now have a good idea how much work you need to do: Are you starting from scratch, or are you already in a good spot? Take this

to heart: More than in any other marriage phase, newlyweds are open to influence and change. The first two years of marriage are usually when communication patterns form. During this time, they remain relatively flexible: There is room for trial and error.

Communication Techniques

A newlywed's biggest and most important hurdle is to learn how to communicate successfully and to find ways to resolve conflict in a constructive fashion. As famous advice columnist Ann Landers has said: "All married couples should learn the art of battle as they should learn the art of making love. Good battle is objective and honest—never vicious or cruel. Good battle is healthy and constructive, and brings to a marriage the principle of equal partnership."

You likely weathered some storms during the wedding planning and maybe even had a few pre-engagement spats, so you already have a communication style.

Your communication style is influenced by a few factors:

■ The communication styles initiated by your parents and practiced by the family in which you grew up.

■ The codes you've observed in other people's families—and even in the media—that you've admired and absorbed.

■ Your natural inclinations—a person is naturally inclined to be either a "condenser," someone who boils down everything to a few short sentences, or an "amplifier," someone who talks in a flurry of descriptive sentences. Some prefer to get to the point immediately, whereas others meander toward the point.

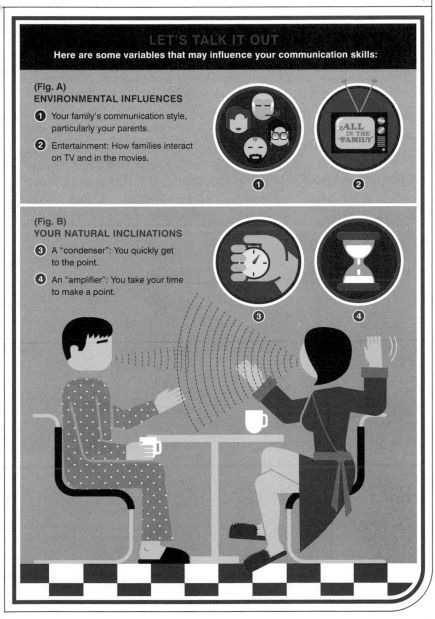

With these points in mind, here are some tips for effective communication.

Acknowledge the differences in your communication styles and recognize that these differences predate your relationship. Be an observer. As you're communicating, notice the nature of your communications. Do any trends emerge? Are any common patterns evident?

Try to communicate in harmony with your spouse's communication style. If you're an amplifier and he's a condenser, you may be drowning him in a sea of words. And you may feel perennially parched from not getting enough water. Recognize that it's an issue, and decide together to adapt your styles to avoid alienating each other.

Ask what your spouse hears you saying. Use a "mirroring" technique. Often what you say is not what the other person hears. The other person hears you through a filter of his or her own making, and sometimes the filter obscures the message. So find out which message is being delivered.

Voice what you think your spouse is saying. Pause and paraphrase what you think your spouse is saying, using "you" sentences. For example, "You're saying that we always talk more about my day than about yours."

If the conversation becomes heated or turns negative, take a break. Don't let negativity breed. Stop and agree to return to the topic after you've had some time away from it.

Focus on appreciation. For every negative comment or complaint, note five positive things about your partner and his or her behavior. This 5-to-1 ratio of appreciation to complaint is one of the recipes for a solid marriage.

Make a request instead of complaining. Again, turn a negative into a positive.
- **Bad:** "You never clean up after dinner."
- **Good:** "How about, when I make dinner, you clean up afterward?"

Avoid sentences that link "you" with "never." See above.

Use positive reinforcement as a form of encouragement (in lieu of nagging).
- **Bad:** "Why don't you ever do anything you say you're going to do?"
- **Good:** "Thank you so much for taking out the trash. It makes coming home so much nicer when the kitchen doesn't stink to high heaven."

Embrace being a yes-man or yes-woman. Before you say no, ask yourself, is this truly an impossibility for me? Can I compromise in order to show my willingness to work as a team?

Some key phrases:
- Yes, dear.
- Happy to help.
- I completely agree.

Potential Problem Areas

Most couples tend to fight about the same things. You're in line with typical newlywed behavior if most of your fights are about the following:

■ **Money** (Saving versus spending, large purchases, spiraling debt, borrowing from family)

■ **In-laws/family** (Over- and underinvolved in-laws and other family members, holiday visitation schedules, needy siblings or other relatives)

■ **Sex** (Varying libidos)

■ **Career** (Time spent at work vs. at home, earning potential and career switches, office husbands and wives)

■ **Religion** (Frequency of visits to house of worship; if you practice different religions, which one to follow, especially once you start thinking about having kids)

How to Fight

Fighting is not an enjoyable activity, but it's impossible to avoid altogether. There's no way that two people will be able to agree all the time. It's highly unlikely that a cohabitating couple will never get on each other's nerves. Studies have shown that the typical couple has nearly 200 arguments per year, and most are over household chores, not listening to each other, or lack of sexual relations. Low blood pressure and fatigue affect the frequency of fights as well—adults are similar to babies in that they grow cranky when tired or hungry. This unhappy state makes them more likely to pick a fight.

There are correct and incorrect ways to argue. The incorrect methods tend to intensify fights and engender hurt feelings. The correct way allows a couple to work through a disagreement positively while treating each other with respect and avoiding juvenile put-downs.

Following are guidelines for friendly fighting:

Do not shy away from conflict. Identifying and acting on differences will allow you to grow your relationship in a way that's satisfying for each partner. If you don't speak up when you're unhappy, the source of that unhappiness will remain and fester like an open sore.

Address the issue, not the person. When you do bring up your gripe, do so within the context of the actual issue. Focusing on the matter at hand allows you to bypass the character assassination that leads to more fights and hurt feelings.

Be a generous listener. This is especially true if your spouse is the person with the complaint. If something is bothering him or her enough to bring it up, he or she deserves your respect and your attention. Listen fully before jumping in with a defensive "But I" or a "You shouldn't," i.e., a negation of your spouse's feelings. Save your point of view until the other person is finished, and try to focus on what is being said instead of formulating a response in your mind while he or she is speaking. (People can tell when you're not really listening.) Sometimes it's enough just for the person to be heard, and the threatening fight never occurs.

Don't turn it around to make it about you. This is the other person's time to speak. Don't consider it the moment to air all grievances, including your own.

Talk softly. Speak at a normal volume—don't raise your voice or shout, since that only adds anxiety, pressure, and drama to a situation that should remain calm and even.

Ask specific questions. This goes a step further than generous listening. Ask specifics about your partner's complaint to come from a place of understanding. Try to break down sentences that start with "You never" or "You always" into specifics. Ask for examples. Instead of jumping to a defensive position, assume a mantle of curiosity. What exactly is bothering your spouse? How can you fix the problem?

Make concessions. As soon as you show you're willing to budge in order to solve the problem, the situation will likely begin to turn around.

Make up. Agree from the outset that making peace is much more important than being right or winning. When you "win" an argument with your spouse, your relationship loses and, in the end, so do you. Even if you feel you've made more concessions during this particular conflict, rest assured it will all even out during your lifetime together.

Put it behind you. Don't hold a grudge. Forgive, forget, and don't bring up this argument to distract from future arguments.

Respect each other's post-fight recovery periods. Some people bounce back immediately into lovey-dovey land. For others, it takes a little time to transition from an intense discussion back into the status quo of daily life.

How to Identify Unfriendly Fighting

Advice for how to fight can often feel abstract, so here are several specific ways to help you know if you're not doing it right:

Global character judgments are made.
Husband: "Why didn't you take out the trash last night?"
Wife: "You're so obsessive-compulsive. I wish you weren't a neat freak like your mother."

Why it's dysfunctional:
- The initial matter goes unaddressed.
- She dodges the issue at hand while delivering a mean-spirited observation that's designed to hurt him.
- His hurt feelings will not make him amenable to future compromise when she raises an issue.

THE MAIN EVENT: Conflict in marriage is inevitable, so you should lear

UNFRIENDLY FIGHTING

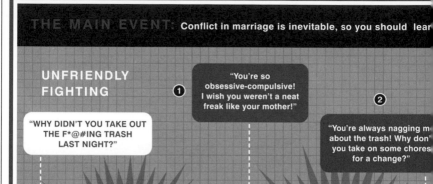

① "You're so obsessive-compulsive! I wish you weren't a neat freak like your mother!"

"WHY DIDN'T YOU TAKE OUT THE F*@#ING TRASH LAST NIGHT?"

② "You're always nagging me about the trash! Why don't you take on some chores for a change?"

③ "Oh, please! How about the time I went away for a week and you forgot to clean the litter box?"

RESULTS:

① The matter goes unaddressed.

② Overgeneralizing and defensiveness occurs.

③ Past events are brought up.

⚠ **CAUTION:**
The following situations are not the proper time or place to have an argument:

Before Bed

While Driving

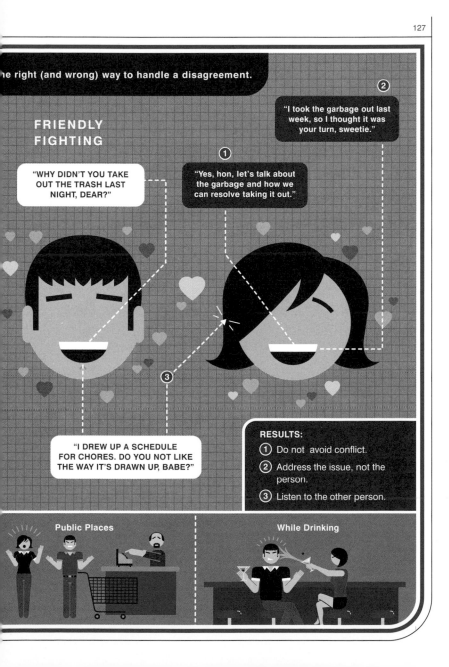

The conversation is peppered with "you should."

Husband: "Why didn't you take out the trash last night?"

Wife: "You should've reminded me it was trash day. You should've had it ready and waiting in the hallway."

Why it's dysfunctional:

■ Again, the initial matter goes unaddressed. Instead, the conversation becomes about what *he* didn't do. She has put him on the defensive instead of answering the question and coming up with a solution together.

Overgeneralizing and defensiveness occurs.

Husband: "Why didn't you take out the trash last night?"

Wife: "You're always nagging me about the trash. Why don't *you* take on some chores for a change?"

Why it's dysfunctional:

■ Things don't *always* or *never* happen, so when you make a statement that includes one of these words, it's just untrue. Claims of *never* and *always* lead to arguments about the frequency of the thing, not the actual specific thing, and this argument is irrelevant.

Past events are brought up.

Husband: "Why didn't you take out the trash last night?"

Wife: "Oh, please. How about the time I went away for a week and you forgot to scoop the litter box?"

Why it's dysfunctional:

■ Now they're arguing about a past event that may or may not have happened, and the complaint has transferred from her to him. She dodged it.

■ She is using the past event to justify the current problem.

Other issues are brought into the conversation.

Husband: "Why didn't you take out the trash last night?"

Wife: "Well, if you didn't make so much trash, it wouldn't have to be taken out so often!"

Why it's dysfunctional:

■ Now the onus is on him to justify his trash output instead of on her to explain why she failed to do the task.

When and Where to Fight

There is a time and a place for fighting, and being able to wait is a good indicator that you're fighting well and not impulsively or explosively. If the right time and place never materialize, go ahead and schedule the discussion.

Timing Dos and Don'ts

■ **Don't** fight right before bedtime. You're probably tired and cranky, and you risk going to sleep angry. Since you won't have time in the morning to make up, the argument will seep far into the following day.

■ **Don't** fight when you have ample time ahead of you, perhaps early evening or on a weekend afternoon.

■ **Don't** fight when you or your spouse is stressed or angry about something else, such as work or family troubles.

- **Don't** fight when either of you has had too much to drink.
- **Do** fight when you've had ample sleep and your appetite is satiated.
- **Do** fight when you have each other's full attention, i.e., not during a must-see football game or TV show or when one of you is preparing a big presentation for work or school.

Physical Location Dos and Don'ts

- **Don't** fight in the car. It makes for hazardous driving and can potentially segue into road-rage incidents. There is no "out" when you're in the car, and sometimes you need to retreat to separate corners when an argument reaches a turning point.
- **Don't** fight in public. No one else wants to hear or see your disagreement. It's difficult to find those separate corners when you're out in public, too.
- **Do** fight while you're both sitting down (but not while you're sitting down in the car—see above). You're more likely to remain calm and relaxed.

Marriage Counseling

Sometimes it's necessary to seek professional help. Society has attached a stigma to relationship counseling, especially for newlyweds who are supposed to be blissfully happy all the time, but most therapists encourage people to have counceling even before getting married. The earlier you learn to communicate effectively, the better. Marital discord takes quite a toll on those who suffer through long, unhappy marriages, and may cause some to die an early death due to the negative health effects from all that stress and strife. Think of counseling as preventive medicine.

LET'S TALK IT OUT

Relationship counseling can help when marital discord rears its ugly head.

BEFORE CHOOSING A THERAPIST:

1. Determine whether your insurance plan covers marriage counseling.
2. Seek recommendations from friends and family.
3. Verify qualifications.

If either of the following conditions applies to your marriage, you should seek a therapist:

- Your quality of life as a couple is bad more often than it's good.
- You seem to repeat the same arguments, and you feel like you have no idea how to stop them.

How to Choose a Therapist

You'll meet for several counseling sessions, during which you'll disclose your innermost thoughts and fears, so make sure the therapist is someone you're comfortable with and respect. Also, therapy is not cheap, so you don't want to hop from one to the next—you'll only be wasting money. Aim to do some work up-front to be certain you've chosen the right therapist for both spouses. A few tips to keep in mind:

Don't go to your spouse's therapist. It's a better idea to find a new and neutral third party who has no preconceived notions of either spouse.

Check your insurance plans. Determine whether you are covered for marriage counseling, for how many sessions, and whether you need a referral from your primary-care physician.

Ask around. As much as you're comfortable, seek recommendations from your friends and family members for therapists in your area.

Verify qualifications. Several suffixes are possible when it comes to counselors. Know your acronyms and degrees: a Ph.D. has a doctorate in something (that may or may not be related to counseling); a Psy.D. has a doctorate in psychology; an M.D. graduated from medical school; a family counselor has had some training in the field of family relations (check extent of training, if that's important to you); someone who's trained in couples therapy will have an M.F.T. certification. If it's not clear, ask during the interview, "What are your credentials?"

Narrow down your choices to a few prospects and then interview them. The one who looks great on paper may not be a match once you're face-to-face. A meeting also gives you a chance to find out more about their experience. Some questions to ask: How long have you been a marriage counselor? What's your philosophy/method of treatment? How many sessions do you suggest for a typical course of treatment? What is your fee?

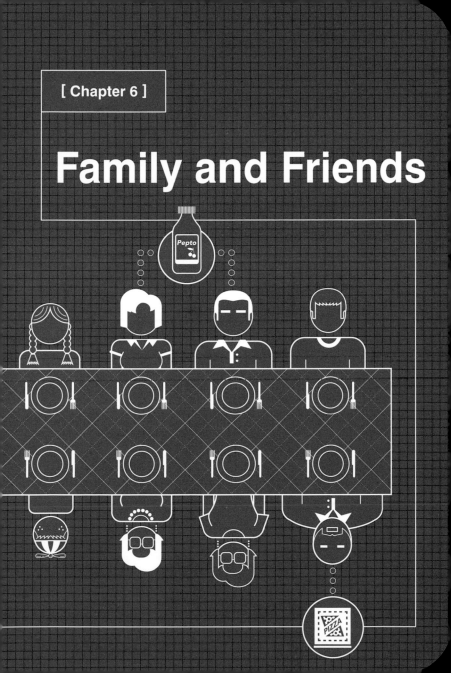

[Chapter 6]

Family and Friends

The In-Laws: Managing Two Different Families

When you marry someone, you marry their family, too, particularly the members to which they're closest. That most often includes their parents, and though you've fully vetted, fallen in love with, and come to terms with your new spouse's unique quirks, you've likely not done the same with his or her parents. You need to take a deep breath, face up to the fact that they're your in-laws now and they'll be your in-laws forever, and then set out to determine how to make that relationship work for you and your marriage.

The Two Laws of In-Laws

No matter the situation, these are the two laws you must return to whenever an in-law issue flares up.

■ **Law #1:** You and your new spouse are a family, and your small, fledgling unit is priority number one.

■ **Law #2:** You and your spouse need to agree to stand together and firm in the face of in-law-induced pressure, guilt, or manipulation, however well intended or skillfully dispatched it may be.

The Mother-In-Law/Daughter-In-Law Relationship

Of all the in-law configurations (MIL/SIL, FIL/DIL, etc.), this relationship is often the most complex and problematic. No one knows exactly why—just that it's often difficult and it can be difficult in a number of ways. You probably have a good idea which type of mother-in-law you're dealing with due to whatever occurred during the wedding planning—a stressful time for a mother-in-law, who must come to terms with the fact that she's about to "lose" her son. Wedding planning often brings out a person's true character. Read the descriptions below to determine which character you're dealing with.

The Smotherer-in-Law: "Call me Mom," is her mating call. Whenever she sees the two of you together, she tears up and then grabs you and envelops you in a bone-crushing embrace that's oftentimes accompanied by swaying and murmuring. She wants to be your mom. She sends you mushy birthday and just-because cards.

■ **Identifiers:** She may not have a daughter of her own. She probably wanted to go shopping with you for your wedding gown.

■ **How to Cope:** Set some boundaries. Maybe you don't return her cards with cards of your own. Maybe you're polite to her and even a little chilly instead of matching her hug for hug. If you don't feel comfortable calling her "Mom," say so.

The Confidante: She wants to be your best friend. She wants to be your ally. She discloses potentially embarrassing information about your spouse's early habits as if to entice you into disclosing similar information about him as an adult. Beware of her motives—she may lull you into thinking you're soul sisters, but her allegiance will always be with her little boy.

■ **Identifiers:** She often flashes you obvious, conspiratorial winks. She friends you on your social-networking site and then comments on every single status update and picture you post.

■ **How to Cope:** Keep your lips sealed. Don't match her disclosure for disclosure. Instead, maintain a warm, slightly detached demeanor that will hopefully let her know you'd rather be your husband's wife than your mom-in-law's daughter-friend.

The Ice Queen: You can't imagine ever calling her "Mom," because if you did, she might fix you with a stare so hard and cold, you'd freeze into an ice sculpture on the spot. When entering your home, she pauses and scans its contents with hard, judging eyes. She may be smiling on the outside, but you get the distinct impression she's certainly not smiling on the inside.

■ **Identifiers:** She dresses impeccably and has a maid service visit her own home twice a week.

■ **How to Cope:** Be the bigger person and find any common ground you can dredge up. Do you both like tulips? Modern art? For the sake of a future that's free of conflict, try your hardest to find something on which you can both agree. You may feel you're doing all the work in this relationship by stretching to find the common ground, and you can feel bitter about that for a short while. Then shake it off. It's for your own good.

The Mom-Wife: She's still very attached to her little boy, so attached that you sometimes wonder if she thinks he's actually her husband. She calls him every day to check in. She calls him whenever she has a problem. She also insists on knowing every little detail of his work- and home-life.

■ **Identifiers:** She may be divorced or widowed.

■ **How to Cope:** Gently bring up to your husband that he seems to talk to his mother an awful lot. (Never let the words "momma's boy" cross your

lips.) Discourage him from answering her every single call, e-mail, and text message. Consider having a third party talk to him about it, since he may not take this advice well coming from you.

The Big-Drama Mama. Everything that happened to her today, yesterday, and, yes, tomorrow, is a HUGE deal, and she must tell you about it now, because you're never going to believe it!!! Her news often overshadows your own, even if it's momentous and exciting news such as your impressive promotion at work. No, her trip to the supermarket that day definitely trumps a promotion.

■ **Identifier:** Strangely enough, she never tries to out-dramatize her son—it's just you.

■ **How to Cope:** She's probably feeling insecure about her standing with her child—your spouse—and she's trying to remind him and everyone else in the room that she's there and that she's important, dammit, so look at her now and everyone needs to stop looking at you.

The Control Freak: Nothing you do is quite right unless you've consulted her on how to do it. She has the right person for you to call for just about everything—and no other person, no matter how great he or she is, will suffice. She pretends to be nonchalant about it, and her digs may be subtle, but if things aren't done her way, she'll never let you forget it.

■ **Identifier:** Lots of raised eyebrows and strongly worded suggestions.

■ **How to Cope:** Limit her visits to times when you're both home. She'll probably be less likely to criticize in front of her son. Counter her suggestions with a dollop of gratitude followed by a firm rejection—"Thanks for the idea. I can see why you did it that way, but this way works best for us and for our family."

Strategies for Avoiding Conflict with Your Mother-in-Law

■ Adopt a positive view of your mother-in-law. Instead of becoming annoyed and focusing on what you consider her negative aspects, think instead about her as the mother of the man you love. She must've done something right in order for your husband to turn into the man you married. This will help you concentrate on good things and minimize problems.

■ When you're angry with your spouse, don't take it out on your mother-in-law. Be careful of directing any anger you may feel toward your husband toward his family.

■ Empathize. Put yourself in her shoes. She did sort of lose a son. Until you came along, she was probably the most important woman in his life. This is probably somewhat difficult and it's a justification for annoying behavior (but probably not for mean-spirited behavior).

■ Avoid comparing your mother-in-law to your own mother and your spouse's family to your own family. Comparisons can lead to defensiveness, rebuttals, unnecessary arguments, and harsh feelings.

The Father-in-Law/Son-in-Law Relationship

A son-in-law is, at worst, a threat and, at minimum, a pain in the butt. Everything's been going along fine. Dad is the king of the castle. And then some new guy shows up and starts basking in loving gazes from the princess in the castle. Hackles immediately raise. Even after a year-long engagement and a wedding, a father-in-law can still be unsure of his new son-in-law. He may still need his son-in-law to prove he's worthy of his daughter. This relationship doesn't get as much ink as the notorious mother-in-law/daughter-in-law pairing, but it can be just as tricky.

Here's what you might be dealing with:

The Master of Your Domain: He surveys everything you do with an eye toward telling you how to do it better or how he did it or whom you should call to have it done. He has advice for every little thing, even when he's not consulted. When he walks into your home, the first thing out of his mouth is an observation that your downpipe is cocked or your windows are too drafty.

■ **Identifier:** An antsy demeanor and a toolkit.

■ **How to Cope:** Pick your battles. Welcome and follow his advice *some* of the time. (After all, he does have more experience and probably some good pointers to share.) For the rest of it, thank him for his wisdom and assure him that you'll consider his suggestions when you get around to fixing/doing whatever.

The Protector: Even though he gave you his blessing to marry his daughter, he's still not sure you're up to the job. He's plenty suspicious of you—not of your motives, since you have made an honest woman out of his daughter—but of your capabilities as a man and as a husband and as the future father of his grandchildren.

■ **Identifier:** He looks at you sideways. He may squint a lot when talking to you.

■ **How to Cope:** He's listening to and observing you closely, so think before you speak or act and ask yourself if what you're about to say or do is appropriate for someone who demands trust and respect.

Strategies for Avoiding Conflict with Your Father-in-Law

The good thing about father–son issues is that, emotionally, men tend to be a little less complicated than women, and therefore most problems are easier to ameliorate. Here are some ways to win over a difficult father-in-law.

■ Do some detective work. Discover his preferred hobbies, TV shows, books, etc., and try to engage him in conversations about his favorite things. Don't go into these discussions pretending you're an expert, or he may lose respect for you. Instead, undertake them with a genuine spirit of curiosity and a willingness to listen and learn.

■ Ask his advice. Even if he doesn't impose his advice on you, like the "Master of Your Domain" type, he probably still wants to offer it and is holding back. He'll be happy to have the unfettered chance to deliver it via your invitation, and he'll look kindly on you for realizing he has wisdom to impart.

■ Don't try to be his buddy. Follow his lead. If he doesn't give you friendly smacks on the shoulder or high-fives, if he doesn't call you "son" or "buddy of mine," don't be overly familiar with him. Some people need to ease into a relationship. He may be uncomfortable with such behavior, and it will only antagonize him more. Be patient. You have years to become friends.

There will be positive benefits for everyone if you develop good relationships with your in-laws. Here are some general strategies for avoiding conflict and building a good relationship.

■ Share the responsibility for maintaining happy relations with both families. Both spouses should sign birthday and holiday cards, offer gifts, send e-mails, plan visits, etc.

■ Treat both families fairly and equally.

■ Try to enhance your spouse's relationship with his or her family. If she's someone who always forgets birthdays, you may want to remind her to send birthday wishes to her parents and siblings. If he never calls his parents, encourage him to do so once in a while.

Inevitable (and Major) In-Law Issues

Holidays

Why They're an Issue:

For some families, holidays are the only times during the year when everyone has a chance to gather together. Families' strongest traditions are also tied to holidays, making it especially disappointing if one family member can't join in the festivities. This situation gets even more complicated when in-laws are divorced and there are four separate parties to please. Still, in-laws need to realize that their married son or daughter can't spend every major holiday with one family at the exclusion of the spouse's family. Newlyweds must split their time between the two families and eventually host holidays on their own.

Solutions:

■ Divvy them up. Interfaith couples often dodge the holiday landmine since rarely do the holidays of major religious coincide. But regardless of your religious backgrounds (or lack there of), certain holidays might be a bigger deal for your families, and the splitting of days could work out if one family does a giant summer party the other year and the other family's big day is New Year's.

■ Alternate. If the solution above won't work, you'll likely have to switch off, spending the holiday with one spouse's family one year and the other spouse's family the next. Once you make your plans clear, then no one can, or should, complain.

■ Make an appearance. If your families live close enough to each other that you can be with both during the holiday, and if all the hopping around doesn't exhaust you to the core, then this strategy might work best for you.

■ Split up. If your families are extra-insistent on your presence and you both have dire reasons for being with your families for a certain holiday, you may have to split up. But try not to do it often. It violates In-Law Law #2: Stand together.

■ Host. If you feel as though you're being stretched like a piece of taffy by both sides and you can't say no to either, host the holiday yourself and invite everyone to come to you.

Visits

Why They're an Issue:

Perhaps your spouse enjoyed frequent visits from parents. Maybe they used to come once a month and sleep on the couch. You're more of a see-your-parents-twice-a-year kind of person. If that's the case, it will surely be difficult for both of you to adapt to the other's parental visitation schedule.

Solutions:

■ Set boundaries. First agree together what those boundaries will be so that you can present a united front to both sets of in-laws. Will you (a) forbid unannounced visits and (b) limit announced visits to once per month? These are the kinds of things you need to decide together. Once you do, stick to your agreement even if one set of parents insists on keeping up pre-marriage rituals.

(Note: Don't place all the blame on your spouse for the reason they can't visit. That lays the groundwork for resentment and bitterness. Use "we," instead of "he" or "she." Example: "We've decided that we really need our weekends to ourselves since we're both working so hard and never see each other during the week.")

■ Move. The ideal distance between your home and your in-law's home is an hour and a half's drive: far enough to discourage unannounced visits yet close enough to allow for free babysitting should that need arise.

Family Vacations
Why They're an Issue:

Your families may have certain vacation traditions. Maybe everyone spends a week together at the family timeshare, or the winter ski trip has been a regular ritual for decades. Combine all the family vacations plus all the holidays, including travel days, and you've eaten up your precious vacation that your workplace allows—and none of it has gone toward your all-important romantic getaway.

Solutions:

■ Set expectations early. Face the problem head-on instead of putting off decisions. Last-minute refusals will disappoint your hosts more than an early, well-explained, well-reasoned "No, thank you, but maybe next year."

Borrowing Money
Why It's an Issue:

One of you may come from a family that doubles as an ATM—whenever you need a cash infusion, it's yours—and the other one may come from a family who has made you work for your allowance since elementary school. These differing attitudes toward money can turn into a sticky scenario when it comes time for a big purchase and one of you wants to borrow, the other doesn't, or one set of in-laws offers a loan, and the other wishes you well and keeps their wallet closed. Any and all of these behaviors can lead to resentment and confusion.

ahead of time with your spouse so you can present a united front.

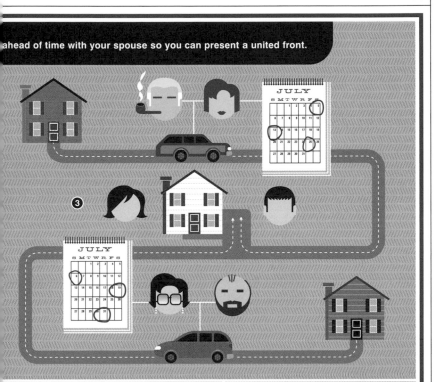

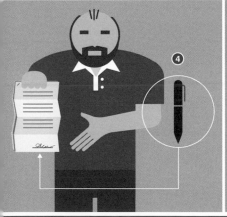

HOLIDAYS:

1. Try to alternate holidays so that you both spend equal time with each spouse's family.

2. Invite both sets of in-laws to *your* home so you can spend time with both families simultaneously.

VISITS:

3. Decide ahead of time with your spouse what the boundaries are and how frequent visits should occur.

BORROWING MONEY:

4. Come up with a repayment plan with your spouse and draw up a contract.

Solutions:

■ Come up with a game plan. With budget in hand, you and your spouse will know how much you'll need for big purchases and when you'll need it. If you want to factor in contributions from your in-laws, decide beforehand and then approach each side. Don't wait for an offer, or you'll be forced to be reactive. Instead, decide what each of you is comfortable asking for and then ask— ideally face to face, with all parties present and with a detailed budget on the table to show your in-laws that you've thought things through.

■ Pay them back. Even if it wasn't your habit to pay back your own parents, now that you're married, resolve to draw up a contract when you borrow any money from either set of in-laws. The contract should include a repayment plan so that there are no questions from either side about when and if the money will be repaid. This type of agreement also helps your in-laws regard you and your spouse as responsible adults who honor their commitments.

Friends: Yours, His, Ours

Just because you're married now doesn't mean all your time needs to be couple-time. On the contrary, you should balance your couple-time with individual time and time with friends (alone and as a couple). That may seem like a lot to work into an already busy schedule, but it's really no different from when you were engaged and, before that, when you were in a committed relationship. Somehow you managed to fit it all in then, and you will, now, too.

Plans with Friends and Visitors

Now that you share a life and a home, you need to establish ground rules regarding making plans and inviting people to your home.

Check with your spouse. To reduce confusion and overscheduling, agree to run all plans by your spouse before confirming anything. The proper response to someone who calls to set up dinner or hanging-out plans is, "Sounds great. I'm going to tentatively say 'yes,' but I need to double-check with [*spouse name*] to make sure we don't already have plans."

Establish regular rituals. Scheduling becomes easier when you have regular commitments in your social schedule. Having standing dates also cuts out the chaotic organizing and planning stages, ensuring that you'll actually see your friends more regularly. This goes for couples-only plans as well as plans with others. Some examples of weekly/monthly/yearly standing engagements might be:

Weekly
- Date night (just the two of you)
- TV night (just the two of you)

Monthly
- Ladies, Guys, or Couples Poker Night
- Game night
- Supper Club (someone hosts a potluck or the group tries out different restaurants)
- Book Group

Yearly

- The annual weekend getaway with the same friends every year
- The annual just-the-two-of-you vacation—duration of and location dependent on financial circumstances

Agree on house rules. When he was a bachelor, he didn't mind if his buddies popped in and lounged on the couch for hours, nursing beers and watching football. A spouse will not usually share the same view on unannounced visits and duration of stays. Talk about it and decide early in your cohabitation what your expectations and limits are as far as short- and long-term houseguests.

Maintaining Friendships and Making Friends

Just because you're married doesn't mean you have to stop dating—oftentimes, making new friends feels a lot like dating. Similarly, maintaining your old friendships after you've become a unit of two can feel like you're in a relationship and trying to keep the romance alive. And how do you blend your two separate groups of friends? What if they're like oil and water?

Make time for old friends. You likely neglected them during the wedding-planning process because you felt like you were holding down two full-time jobs. Now that you have a bit more free time on your hands, use it to rekindle old friendships. (This is also a good time to assess your friendships and decide which ones you want to rekindle and which ones you wouldn't mind leaving stagnant.)

Reach out to your spouse's friends. You probably met some of them at the wedding or at parties surrounding the wedding, but since you were the center of attention, you didn't have much opportunity to pause and get to know them. Make plans with them soon after returning from your honeymoon.

Play matchmaker. Think about who would get along among your respective groups of friends and throw some dinner parties to test possible combinations. The more you're able to successfully blend and merge your circles, the easier it will be for you to socialize more often with the people you like.

Don't force it. Just because you're married doesn't mean your groups of friends must like one another. If there are some bad matches in the group, don't force the situation by constantly throwing them together. Eventually they just won't show up. Similarly, if you've tried to like one of your spouse's friends but just can't seem to get along, don't push your significant other into giving up that friend. Instead, make concurrent plans with people you do like.

Court new friends. Maybe you're the first among your friends to get married, so you're starved for couple friends. You've moved into a new neighborhood, and the couple two doors down seems to have great pal potential. Don't suffocate or stalk them. Instead, try to bump into them nonchalantly. During these brief, happenstance meetings, determine if they share common interests. Do they like the same bars, restaurants, music, TV shows, political figures? If not, don't force it. If so, ask if they'd like to grab brunch or a drink in the neighborhood sometime.

Remain true to your single friends. When socializing with single friends, keep an eye on your "we-ness." Stick with the pronoun "I" as much as possible.

That also goes for sentences that start with, "As my husband/wife always says . . . " You have plenty to talk about besides your spouse and your couple-heavy activities. There's work, current events, the weather, movies, books, mutual friends, their dating life, future travel, etc.

Entertaining

You probably entertained when you were single and when you were dating, too, but hosting parties and houseguests is different once you're married. There's no identifiable reason why. It's due to some combination of you now having china; coordinating glassware and dishes; possibly a big, new space in which to entertain; and two guaranteed hosts instead of one.

When you each entertained individually, you probably had different styles. How do you meld them? First you need to determine which category you each fall into:

Casual entertainer: You announce impromptu parties the day before or the day of, and encourage everyone to bring food and drinks, in addition to organizing and setting up and maybe going for a quickie supermarket/liquor store run. If the house is a little dirty, so be it. Your priority is seeing people, people seeing each other, hanging out, and having fun.

Constant entertainer: You hate being alone and, in fact, encourage everyone and anyone to drop by and pop in whenever they're in the neighborhood. You always have snacks on hand, stacks of board games at the ready, a giant BBQ in your backyard, and a special refrigerator for your kegerator.

Occasional entertainer: Entertaining is not your forte. Something about it turns you off. Maybe you don't like groups of people—you prefer to interact one-on-one. Maybe you're intimidated by the thought of preparing for a party, something about it—the decorating, the cleaning, the cooking, the hiring of a caterer—makes you break out in hives.

Painstaking entertainer: You may as well write books about entertaining because you're that skilled at it. You dream up innovative theme parties that thrill your guests; you make charming and funny conversation; and you effortlessly mingle among your guests, introducing them to one another and then flitting on to the next group. Your china always sparkles. Your food always pleases. You make it look easy, but you actually put plenty of work into each of your fetes, because everything has to be absolutely perfect.

Some of these types blend together better than others. A casual and a constant entertainer won't need to adjust their styles too much to be in line with each other, but they may find that the house is overrun with people all the time. After a few months, assess the situation and stop putting out the welcome mat should you decide the nonstop parade of freinds is a problem. An occasional entertainer will find living with a painstaking entertainer a little easier than living with a casual entertainer, since the latter probably entertains infrequently, too. If an occasional entertainer winds up with a constant entertainer, however, both sides are going to have to adjust their lifestyles and their expectations. They should try to meet somewhere in the middle and/or move into a house with a soundproofed wing so that the occasional entertainer can opt out of the constant parties.

How to Entertain

Once you decide to entertain, your options are nearly unlimited. There's a long list of types of parties and events that you can host and throw: holiday parties (Halloween costume parties, Easter egg hunts, New Year's Eve parties); parties around food (dinner parties, wine and cheese tastings, cooking parties); and parties that just last for an hour or two (cocktail parties, brunches, book club meetings). Here are some how-tos for three basic types of parties: the dinner party, the cocktail party, and poker night.

Dinner Party

Whom to Invite:
■ Two to four people who already know and like one another or will certainly like one another once they meet. Your goal is to pick a group for whom conversation will flow easily.

What You Need:
■ A theme: Not required, but it makes entertaining easier. (Sample themes include: sports events, holidays, cooking, movie or book oriented, cultural celebrations, and TV shows.)
■ Food
■ A signature drink (again, not required, but makes entertaining easier since you'll need only one or two types of liquor)
■ Wine, beer, and a nonalcoholic beverage

Hosting Tips:
■ Prepare as much as possible before the party. That includes cleaning, setting the table (or at least taking inventory of what you'll need and making

sure everything's clean and within reach), food preparation, outfit selection, inserting the leaf in the dining table, etc.

■ Divvy up assigned duties with your spouse. Who's going to keep people's glasses filled and refreshed? Who's going to take coats? Who's going to serve as DJ?

■ Have a glass of wine or a cocktail an hour before everyone arrives, to calm your nerves, but try not to indulge too much once guests arrive.

Cocktail Party

Whom to Invite:

■ Fifteen to twenty friends

What You Need:

■ A signature drink (see previous page, under "Dinner Party")

■ Wine, beer, and nonalcoholic beverage options

■ Finger foods—several plates of hors d'oeuvres, crackers and cheese, crudités and dips

■ Music

Hosting Tips:

■ Don't try to provide every drink for every person. Narrow the choices to one or two cocktails, wine, and beer. Or just wine and beer.

■ Remember to have one or two nonalcoholic choices, plus water.

■ Check at least a week before that you have all the hard-to-find "hardware" on hand—stemware, cocktail napkins, napkin holders, ice bucket and tongs, etc. Actually put your hands on the items you're planning to use to serve the food and alcohol or you run the risk of thinking you have something when you actually don't. You don't want to spend the day before the

Entertaining 101: Throwing a great party to entertain friends can be great fun

PARTY TYPE:

WHOM TO INVITE:

DINNER PARTY

Two to four people

COCKTAIL PARTY

Fifteen to twenty friends

POKER NIGHT

Three to six players

ut you need the know-how to pull it off. Here are some how-tos for three party types.

WHAT YOU NEED:	HOSTING TIPS:
theme (sports, movies, holidays, etc.)	**Prepare as much as possible before the party.**

usic, finger foods, and a signature drink	**Provide nonalcoholic drinks as well.**

Beer is a staple; cigars are optional	**Don't serve messy foods that could mark the cards—stick with pretzels and nuts.**

party driving from store to store, trying to locate the perfect chip-and-dip set you could've sworn someone gave you as a wedding present.

■ If you're mixing groups (his poker friends with her book-group friends, for example), make sure you've invited a few outgoing personalities who are guaranteed to break the ice.

■ If neither of you are good cooks, there's no shame in buying prepared foods. Do that rather than putting out a bowl of chips and shrugging to people that you're just not talented in the kitchen. You have a responsibility as a host to provide cocktails and tasty snacks, so you should do so (especially if you want people to come to your next party).

Poker Night

Whom to Invite:

■ You can play poker with as few as three and as many as six. (Make sure at least one or two in the group know how to play so that they can school the rest of the players.)

■ Only invite people who like playing poker. If they're not interested in the evening's primary activity, they may distract the other players with their chattiness.

What You Need:

■ Rules: How much is the ante? Decide beforehand by considering how much your guests can afford to lose. You might want to make the ante a penny or a nickel or even a nonmonetary item, like peanuts or beans.

■ Cards

■ Poker chips

■ Pretzels, potato chips, and other snacks

- Beer or other beverages
- Cigars (optional)

Hosting Tips:

- Don't invite more than ten players (including you). You can't play Texas Hold 'Em with more than ten. (Though you can play with as few as three.)
- If there are poker novices in the group, provide printouts that illustrate the hierarchy of winning hands. (This also prevents debates about what beats what.)
- Don't serve anything mushy or messy that might mark the cards. Not only is it unfortunate to soil the cards, but an ace with a chocolate smudge can change the dynamics of the game. (Some no-muss choices are pretzels, dry-roasted nuts, and veggies and dip.)
- Don't invite anyone who's notorious for being super-competitive, since he or she may ruin the fun.

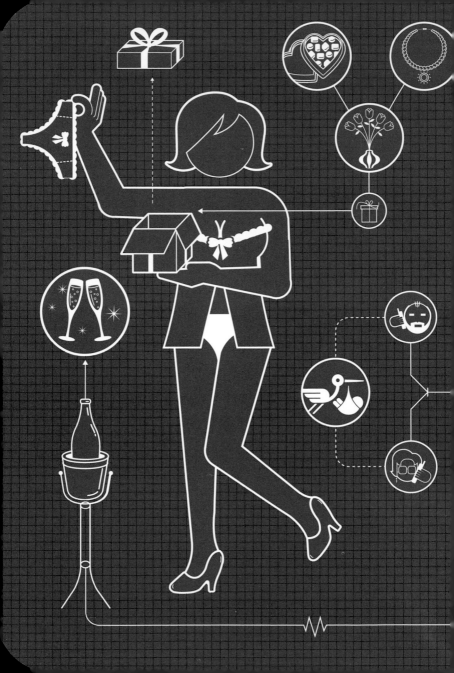

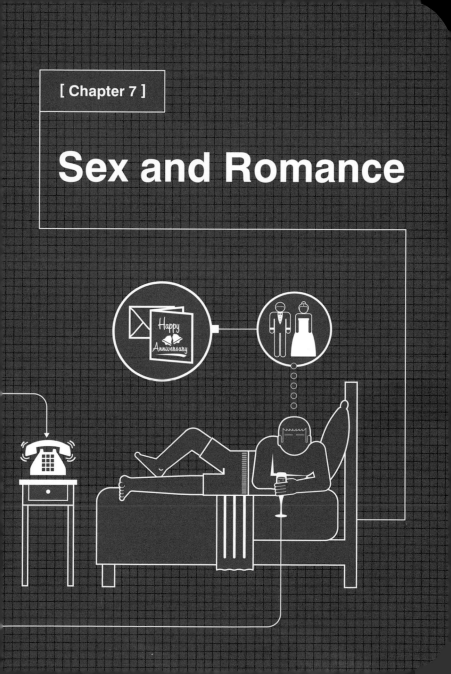

Chapter 7

Sex and Romance

Your marriage partner is supposed to be your best friend and your best lover. How do you maintain the "bests" of both worlds when you're seeing this person every day? You can't re-create the tone of the relationship as it existed in its early, exciting days, when everything was new. Married couples have to work harder to keep the flame lit.

Sex

Sex is one of the most frequent sticking points for married couples—even if both agree it should happen, they may disagree on how often and how to keep it interesting once it's been happening the same way for a long time. The key to resolution is to keep the lines of communication open. Even if you can't fix the problem, it helps to talk about it and to make it known that there is a problem. Even better: Be proactive so that it doesn't turn into a problem in the first place. That is your best marriage insurance policy.

Navigating Different Sex Styles

What's your sex style? Do your individual styles match, or are they out of sync? Two elements define one's sex style: frequency and preferred degree of novelty. Where do you each fall on the following continuums?

Frequency Continuum
Once a month
Once a week
Three times a week
Five times a week

Novelty Continuum
Always the same way, same place
75/25 old/new
About 50/50
Never the same way

Now that you know each other's preferences, what's next?

[1] Talk about it. If you're far apart in terms of the frequency and the degree to which you like to switch things up, you may need to strategize ways to meet in the middle.

Through a frank discussion, you'll ensure that any hurt feelings or misconceptions are dealt with and smoothed over. For example, a partner who is at the high end of the frequency continuum may feel rejected by the partner who's at the low end. A whole host of misunderstandings can ensue. The discussion needs to take place during which the low-frequency partner explains the real reason for the decreasing sex drive. Maybe he or she finds it difficult to switch gears into sex mode because of stress over work, money, or health-related problems. Dig and you may find other underlying issues that need to be addressed.

[2] Lay out your expectations. Decide together what each of you can manage so that both are satisfied. Come up with a plan that might include some or all of the following components:

■ **Frequency:** If you are at separate ends of the continuum, can you compromise on once or twice a week? This number won't dictate your sex life for the rest of your lives. If one of you is still dissatisfied, resolve to see how this decision goes first before reevaluating a few weeks or months down the road.

■ **Timing:** Your frequency levels may just be off because one of you always wants to have sex exactly when the other is least interested. For example, some people are active at night, whereas others just want to wind down and go to sleep. One of you may prefer to have sex in the late afternoon, but have you shared this inclination with your spouse? Talk about times of day and what works best for you to ensure that the frequency you agreed upon will fit with those times when you're most likely to be ready for sex.

■ **Variety:** It is the spice of some people's lives but not of others. Decide how much you'd like to spice up your sex lives and then come up with a general outline for how. Of the twice a week you agreed upon, will one time always be somewhere outside the bedroom? Will you try a different position at least once a week? Again, if your styles are out of sync, compromise and meet in the middle. Start gradually. You can always reassess and ramp things up (or slow things down).

[3] Mark your calendars. A physical reminder will help you see exactly how sex fits into your lives and prioritize it when you're comparing it directly to other tasks in your planner, such as "night out with the girls" and "clean kitchen." (Sex should be at least equal with, if not more important than, these two examples!) Decide together that only emergencies can upstage your sex appointments. (And come up with a good code name for them, such as "salsa lessons" or "cooking class.") Seeing a sex appointment on your calendar will help you prepare mentally for the occasion as well.

[4] Keep your appointments. Getting into the habit will help you eventually increase the frequency and pleasure derived from your "salsa lessons" (or whatever you kids are calling it these days). You're more likely to be spontaneous. Studies have shown that people desire sex more once they have it more often.

Roadblocks

Even the best-laid plans—and relationships—hit roadblocks. The obstacles that litter this particular path are sensitive ones and must be handled carefully. Here are a few issues and suggestions for how to deal with them:

You find porn. There's a stash of magazines in the closet; you walk in on your spouse surfing porn sites online; your cable bill reveals that someone rented *Jugs Across America*. You should definitely speak up and not keep quiet for fear of embarrassment. Porn is nothing to be ashamed of—it's a way to get to know and understand your partner's sexual appetite and preferences. Use this opportunity to open up a dialogue: How often do you watch or look at porn? Why do you like that? Etc.

You have trouble asking for what you want. She's been pulling the same moves in the same places, and what she thinks are your pleasure spots are actually just dead zones. To let her know what you want, you're going to have to speak up, and that isn't always easy. Here are a few ways to go about it:

- Ask what *she* wants. That'll give her the idea to turn around and do the same. (And you should probably be doing this, anyway.)
- Segue into it with some positive reinforcement. When she does something that feels good, say, "Oh, that feels so good. You know what else would feel great?"

One of you is more experimental than the other. If one partner shies away from the introduction of toys and positions, ease into your experimental ways gradually. Consider visiting a sex shop together or looking at them together

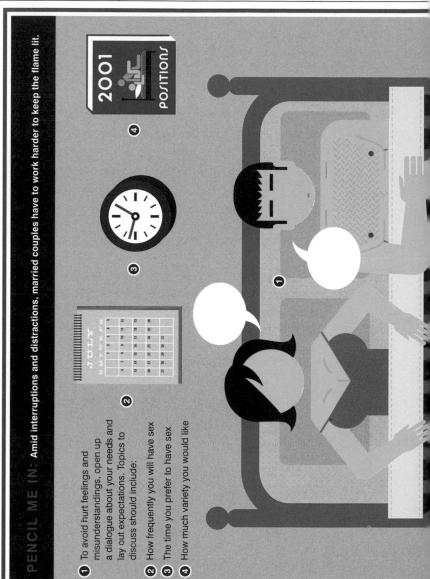

PENCIL ME IN: Amid interruptions and distractions, married couples have to work harder to keep the flame lit.

① To avoid hurt feelings and misunderstandings, open up a dialogue about your needs and lay out expectations. Topics to discuss should include:

② How frequently you will have sex

③ The time you prefer to have sex

④ How much variety you would like

169

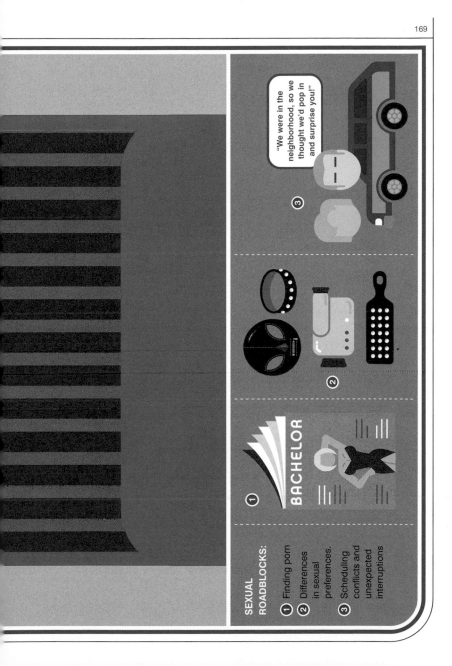

SEXUAL
ROADBLOCKS:

① Finding porn

② Differences
in sexual
preferences.

③ Scheduling
conflicts and
unexpected
interruptions

online at an e-commerce site. That way, you can talk about them and decide together what to try. Keep these discussions light and positive so that your reluctant partner doesn't feel pressured or intimidated.

Your spouse wants to keep a "salsa lesson" appointment, but it falls during a visit to your in-laws. If one of you doesn't feel comfortable in this situation—if the thought of your in-laws walking in on you is distressing rather than exciting—your spouse should make an exception to the usual regimen and agree to postpone the bedroom rendezvous until later.

Romance

Getting married shouldn't mean that two people stop courting each other. All the rituals of courtship—thinking about each other, going out of the way to surprise the other with thoughtful gifts and gestures, giving someone a hug or kiss or flowers just because—should continue even after you say "I do."

The Little Things

Grand gestures are wonderful, but we can't all afford spontaneous trips to Paris or regular gifts of fine jewelry. However, a sustained practice of day-to-day romantic details is what really makes for a strong and loving relationship. Here are some examples of details that you can throw into the mix of your daily lives.

Pass notes. Leave each other thoughtful, funny, silly, loving messages around the house or spontaneously e-mail or text each other during the day

KEEP BRINGING ON THE LOVE

Just because the honeymoon is over doesn't mean the romance needs to end.

KEEPING THE ROMANCE ALIVE:

1. Send her flowers.
2. Leave little notes or texts for him.
3. Surprise her with a gift.
4. Take him out for a romantic dinner.

saying, "I love you," "I miss you," "I think you're amazing," anything to make the other person smile.

Unexpected dates. In addition to designating a date night when the two of you will either go out or stay in to spend time together (i.e., not to work), initiate some surprise occasions for sweeping your spouse out of the house for a fun evening on the town when it's least expected. (Make sure the time is good for both of you, i.e., that your spouse doesn't have a big work deadline the next day.)

Flowers, chocolates, greeting cards. Even clichéd gestures can be effective when they're wielded with the right amount of irony and charm. They work especially well if your spouse loves flowers or has frequent cravings for sweets. As for the greeting card, find the cheesiest, silliest one to give to your spouse "just because."

Little gifts. A small token goes a long way when it transmits the message that you were thinking about your loved one and "better" half.

Make each other laugh. That was one of your goals while you were dating, and it should be now as well. Married dialogue can easily become reduced to discussions about the house, your careers, your in-laws, etc. Be sure to also talk about funny or pleasant things that happened during your day or relay the kinds of interesting anecdotes you made an effort to tell while you were dating.

The Big Things

It's also important to be vigilantly thoughtful when it comes to your relationship. Although the little things add sweet touches, the big things are where it really counts. Make it a point to concentrate on these things:

Help out. It's no coincidence that polls reveal that married women find coming home to discover their spouse has cleaned the house, done the laundry, or taken out the trash without having to be reminded to be super sexy and romantic. Being proactive about doing your fair share of work around the house that you now own together is considered a thoughtful—and even a romantic—gesture.

Pay each other compliments. Try to say something nice to your spouse, about your spouse, every day. It shows that you're not taking the other person for granted, reminding yourself not to do so. If you have to pay a compliment a day, you're forced to watch closely for things to compliment (outfit, efficient morning routine, fresh breath). A good way to remember to say something nice is to add the sentiment to every time you say thank you: "Thank you, it was so nice of you to make dinner tonight," or "Thanks for running out to pick up milk. You always go the extra mile."

Note: Never criticize each other in public. Even if you're in the middle of a spat when you leave the house, don't bring it with you. Criticizing or teasing your spouse in front of friends (and strangers) is a betrayal of your relationship.

Prioritize your relationship. Don't let outside influences derail your relationship. When something comes up that may conflict with an activity you've scheduled together, discuss it first and let your spouse know that he or she comes first.

Anniversaries

Once you're married, you'll need to decide which anniversaries you want to continue celebrating. You may already celebrate a first-date anniversary. Couples often have other anniversaries, too, like a first-kiss anniversary and an engagement anniversary. If you can let some of these others go, it'll make your wedding anniversary that much more special.

Your anniversary is a great excuse to plan something meaningful and romantic for just the two of you. It doesn't have to be complex and over-the-top—maybe you return to the restaurant where you had your first date or even to the place where you married. Bigger anniversaries, such as the tenth or twentieth, deserve bigger treatments, but the first few can be more low-key, especially since most of your money is probably going into mortgage payments or savings accounts.

As for presents, you both should buy gifts for the other—this is a relationship of equals, after all. And the present *must* be romantic—no household appliances, no matter how much she says she wants a new washing machine or he wants that shiny tool.

ANNIVERSARY GIFTS

Here's a list of traditional anniversary gifts and their modern counterparts.

FIRST ANNIVERSARY:

Traditional: **PAPER**

Artwork; a photograph in a nice frame; a book of poetry; a first edition of a book he or she loves; tickets to a performance; monogrammed stationery; a handmade book of highlights of your life together.

Modern: **CLOCKS**

Choose from the many unique clocks and timepieces on the market.

ALSO: Remember to eat the top tier of your wedding cake you've been saving in your freezer for just this moment.

SECOND ANNIVERSARY:

Traditional: **COTTON**

A luxurious high-thread-count robe; a tapestry or other woven work; table or bed linens.

Modern: **CHINA**

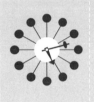

A service piece that matches your china.

THIRD ANNIVERSARY:

Traditional: **LEATHER**

A monogrammed briefcase; a designer handbag; a wallet; gloves; special-occasion shoes.

Modern: **CRYSTAL**

A crystal vase or bowl; a pair of crystal champagne glasses; a prism to hang in the window.

FOURTH ANNIVERSARY:

Traditional: **FLOWERS**

A membership to the flower-of the-month club; a tree to plant in your backyard; a beautiful bouquet; a piece of jewelry designed in the shape of a flower.

Modern: **APPLIANCES**

It is inadvisable to go with the "modern" option for this anniversary.

FIFTH ANNIVERSARY:

Traditional: **WOOD**

A piece of furniture; a wood-carving; a perfume or cologne with a woodsy fragrance; a chessboard; a Scrabble board; vacation in the woods at a log cabin.

Modern: **SILVERWARE**

An antique silver platter or vegetable dish; silver monogrammed napkin rings.

SIXTH ANNIVERSARY:

Traditional: **IRON**

A wrought-iron sculpture for the garden; a wrought-iron bed-frame; a set of golf clubs.

Modern: **WOOD**

A sculpture, piece of furniture or wood carving.

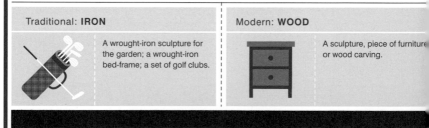

SEVENTH ANNIVERSARY:

Traditional: WOOL

A cashmere throw, a blanket or socks; a sweater.

Modern: DESK SETS

A leather or modern desk set, depending on the recipient's aesthetic preferences.

EIGHTH ANNIVERSARY:

Traditional: BRONZE

Bronze statue, jewelry, or bookends; a sundial for the garden.

Modern: LINEN AND LACE

A lacy negligee, a piece of linen clothing; bed or table linens.

NINTH ANNIVERSARY:

Traditional: POTTERY

Vase, tableware, or serveware; a sculpture.

Modern: LEATHER GOODS

(See "Third Anniversary: Traditional")

TENTH ANNIVERSARY:

Traditional: TIN

Coffee tins, puzzle tins, pressed-tin tiles.

Modern: DIAMOND JEWELRY

A ring with a bigger diamond to replace the original engagement ring, a solitaire necklace, earrings, or a bracelet.

Fun, Cheap, and Creative Date Ideas

You'll need an inventory of activity ideas in order to plan all of those date nights meant to keep the spark alive. Though sometimes the best thing to do is stay at home and snuggle with a movie rental and take-out, there are plenty of ways to get out and about without spending a lot of money. Let's face it: One thing newlyweds don't usually have a lot of is expendable income.

Here are some ideas:

- Go ice skating/roller skating.
- Rent bikes.
- Go hiking.
- Find a free concert.
- Check out a street fair or county fair.
- Go antiquing or flea marketing (and don't buy anything).
- Go to a museum or two.
- Peruse some art galleries in the nearest city or local art district.
- Read poetry to each other.
- Revisit old times—go back and re-create some of your earliest dates, when you were trying really hard to impress each other.
- Play board games.
- Take a dance lesson—then practice at home.
- Prepare a meal together.

The possibilities are endless, so there's no excuse not to spend quality time together and grow as a couple—without breaking the bank.

Offspring

There's a common song about marriage that goes, "First comes love, then comes marriage, then comes so-and-so in a baby carriage." In a nutshell, this is the typical process many couples undergo: After marriage, they begin to think about if and when they want to have children. Many in-laws begin to ask about the possibility of grandchildren even before your wedding. Despite all the societal and familial pressures, you should not feel rushed into making this major life-altering decision.

Figuring Out If You're Ready

First, determine if you, as a couple, are ready for this big life change. You've just been through a major transition by getting married, so you may want to take some time to figure out your own identity as husband and wife. Still, even if the day you want to start trying is a long way away, you should have the conversation early to determine how many (if any) children you want to have and roughly when you want to welcome them into the world. How do you know when you're ready?

Money. You'll need enough to be able to support a baby and all that comes along—healthcare, clothing, food, toys, crib, stroller, nursery gear, etc., and eventually daycare and school.

Career. Where are you in your careers and where are you headed? Is either of you ready to take some time off work—at least three months for maternity leave and several weeks for paternity leave? If she thinks she wants to be a stay-at-home mom, is she ready to take a few years away from the workday world, and can you afford that? Or is the father going to stay at home with the child? If not, can you afford regular daycare and/or a nanny?

Support system. Does your family live nearby? Or friends who can help with the baby? It helps to have a close support system in place, especially if you don't think you'll be able to take a few months or a year off work or if you both have demanding careers.

Age. Fertility in women is thought to decline at age twenty-seven, although every year the birth rate for women in their forties increases. You'll have no idea how easy or difficult it is to get pregnant until you start trying—it's impossible to know whether it's going to take weeks, months, or years.

Relationship. Being married is hard work, and being married with kids is even harder work. You'll need to be on the same page about the division of labor (i.e., chores); the primary caregiver during the week and on the weekends; switch off getting up for nighttime feedings and changing diapers, etc.

Space. Does your current living situation have enough room for a nursery or space for a child to run free? If not, will you be able to afford to move to a bigger house when you need to?

Independence. Do you love to travel? Do the two of you frequently take off on daytrips or weekend jaunts at a moment's notice? This type of lifestyle is unsustainable once you have a baby. Of course, there are many wonderful things about having a child, but if you're not ready to let go of your independence, you may want to think hard about it before diving in.

If You Disagree

Ideally, you should've discussed the family situation before tying the knot, but if you didn't (or if your spouse's opinion has changed), here's what you should know. It can strain a marriage if one partner is ready for kids but the other isn't. Pressuring the person isn't going to change anyone's mind and will only lead to resentment.

Be patient. Accept that your spouse is on a different time line. Perhaps overwhelmed by the transition from being single to being married, he or she may need some time to get used to the new status before moving on to the next big thing. Resolve to bring up the discussion again in a few months, but, until then, give your partner some breathing room.

Arrange visits from cute kids. If any of your friends have children that are particularly adorable or well behaved, make plans for a visit. Increasing your unwilling partner's exposure to exceptional children just might change even the most stubborn mind.

Be honest. Never try to trick your partner into having kids before he or she is ready. Always be open about your wants and desires, and if you can't come to an agreement over many months, consider making an appointment with a marriage counselor to talk about it with an impartial third party.

How to Reply to Pressure from Family to Procreate

In-laws are notorious for not observing the "newlywed buffer," or the time unofficially allotted to every newly married couple during which they should be left alone to enjoy being married (or at least to hammer out the terms of said marriage before they start trying to have kids). Unfortunately many in-laws and other family members have no respect for the buffer, and they launch their offensive as soon as the honeymoon's over, with a constant refrain of, "When? When? When?" Newlyweds should probably expect such behavior from in-laws who don't yet have grandchildren and nip this nagging in the bud by enforcing boundaries right away. Here are some ways to do so.

Phoniness, with sugar on top. "We so appreciate your interest in our lives, but right now we don't have any plans to have kids. You, however, will be among the first to know as soon as we do!"
The Message: Step off. We'll have kids when we're good and ready. (Smile, smile, wink, wink.)

Shock them into submission. "Gosh golly, we would love to have a kid, but we just don't know how babies are made. Could you draw a picture for us?"
The Message: It's none of your business what happens between our sheets.

An honest plea to be left alone. "We know you're anxious for a grandchild, but this decision is very important and it's one that we need to make on our own without any input. We would appreciate it if you gave us some space."
The Message: Don't call us. We'll call you.

THE PRESSURE IS ON!

Every newlywed couple experiences the inevitable baby-making pressure.

(Fig. A)
Be prepared for in-laws without grandchildren to start inquiring about your plans for having kids.

(Fig. B)
Here are a few ways ways to react when you're facing baby-making pressure:

Reaction: **PHONINESS**	Reaction: **PLAYING DUMB**	Reaction: **BACK OFF!**
This says "thanks, but we're not quite ready yet."	This tells them that what happens in the bedroom stays there!	Don't call us. We'll call you.

HAVING KIDS IS SERIOUS BUSINESS

Here are some things to consider before having children:

① ② ③

PREPPING FOR OFFSPRING:

① Start saving money.

② Consider genetic testing before trying to conceive.

③ Women should ask their doctor about taking prenatal vitamins.

④ Determine if daycare is an option or if one parent can stay home with the child.

Preparing for Offspring

Save money. The cost of raising a child from birth to age seventeen is estimated to be a little more than $250,000 for families living in the Midwest on a combined income of around $70,000 per year. It's not necessary to save that much before you begin trying to conceive, but the number gives you a good idea of the costly nature of child-rearing. Make sure you have a buffer in your savings account and that you and your partner have merged your finances in a way that works for your household.

Get tested. Think about genetic testing before trying to conceive. Some ethnicities including Ashkenazi Jews are prone to passing on specific disorders to their children, and testing will indicate whether or not you're a carrier.

Take vitamins. Females should ask their gynecologist for a prescription for prenatal vitamins and start popping them a few months before trying to conceive.

Talk about childcare. Make sure it's clear who's going to opt out of their career for a while and who's not. One of you will need to do so unless you have enough money to pay for an all-day daycare facility and/or a full-time nanny.

Fertility

There is a great deal of information available about fertility, but your best resource is probably your doctor. He or she knows your medical history and is familiar with your past and current conditions. Consult your trusted physician for specifics about fertility and how they relate to you. To get started, here are some general facts:

■ The average couple takes between four and six months to conceive, and for many couples it can take longer.

■ One in six couples cannot conceive without medical intervention, but 90 percent do conceive eventually.

■ Men are equally as likely as women to be the cause of infertility.

■ Experiencing infertility can be very stressful and cause anxiety and depression, so be sure to take extra care of yourself and your spouse if you're having trouble conceiving.

■ Women are most fertile during the ovulation phase of their menstrual cycle.

Fertility can be adversely affected by:

■ STDs

■ Various health problems (for example, having the mumps during adolescence can decrease sperm production)

■ Exposure to radiation

■ Age (A 29-year-old woman has a 20 percent chance of getting pregnant each month; that number decreases to 7 percent for a 39-year-old woman.)

Care and Maintenance of Each Other

Newlyweds have sworn to be partners in sickness and in health, and even if they don't utter those exact vows, the general deal with marriage is that you take care of each other.

You already have an advantage over your former bachelor and bachelorette selves since research shows that married people live longer than single people. The reasons likely have to do with social isolation and with spouses influencing each other's habits. For example, if a woman is used to eating fast food and frozen pizza for every meal, her new husband can drastically improve her health just by preparing a home-cooked dinner a few times a week. By its very nature, a home-cooked meal will be lower in cholesterol and calories. Here are some other ways to keep each other in peak health and top form.

■ Be tobacco free. (Help each other kick the smoking habit.)

■ Exercise and/or be physically active together. (You don't need to go to the gym every day. Rather, once in a while choose to walk instead of driving to the store. It's more fun with a buddy.)

■ Eat healthful foods. Be each other's check and balance and make sure you're mixing in plenty of vegetables, fruit, whole grains, and unprocessed foods.

■ Maintain a healthy weight. Balance your caloric intake with physical activity. Newlyweds often gain a "freshman 15" for several reasons: The pressure to look good for the wedding is off, and you often eat for two now that you're preparing meals for two.

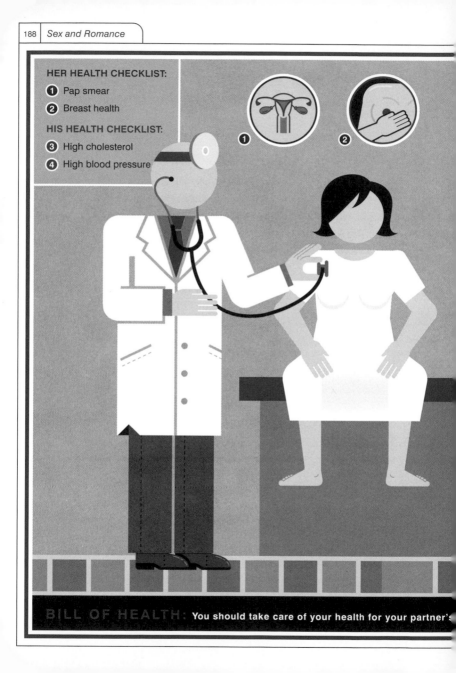

HER HEALTH CHECKLIST:
1. Pap smear
2. Breast health

HIS HEALTH CHECKLIST:
3. High cholesterol
4. High blood pressure

BILL OF HEALTH: You should take care of your health for your partner's

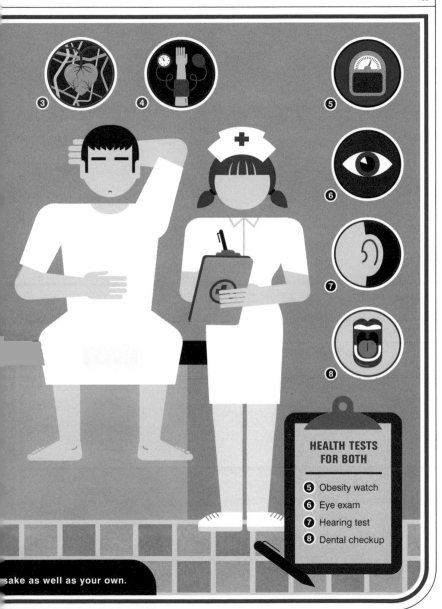

**HEALTH TESTS
FOR BOTH**

5 Obesity watch
6 Eye exam
7 Hearing test
8 Dental checkup

sake as well as your own.

- Help each other stay away from illegal drugs.
- Encourage each other to drink alcohol only in moderation. That means no more than two drinks per day.
- Help each other manage stress.

His Health

Men are notorious for refusing to go to the doctor. No sound theory exists to explain why. Fear of death? Perhaps. Unwillingness to undress in front of a stranger? Possibly. For whatever reason, the reluctance exists and it's often up to the spouse to make sure he sees a doctor for the following basic screening tests:

- High cholesterol: Should be checked every year starting at age 35. Men younger than 35 should have their cholesterol checked if they have diabetes or high blood pressure, if heart disease runs in their family, or if they smoke.
- High blood pressure: Should be checked at least every two years.
- Prostate health: Should be checked starting at age 40.
- Colorectal cancer: Get tested for it regularly, starting at age 50. If there's a family history of colorectal cancer, you may need to be screened earlier.

Her Health

Women are notorious for ignoring their own health to focus on their partner's and eventually on their children's. This is an extra incentive for a newlywed to pay the utmost attention to his new wife's health. Here's a screening-test checklist for her:

- Thyroid: Check every five years, starting at age 35.
- Breast health: Regular self-exams; mammograms once a year starting at age 40.
- Pap smear: Every one to three years.
- Pelvic exam: Annually.

Our Health

These are tests that both spouses should schedule regularly:

- General health: A full physical check-up is advised at least every two years.
- Obesity: If you think you're overweight, ask your doctor to test your body mass index (BMI) to be sure.
- Eyes: Every two years.
- Ears: Every three years.
- Dental checkup: Once or twice a year.
- Skin exam: Monthly self-exams (this is when it comes in handy to live with someone who can check your back for you); and also by your doctor as part of a general routine checkup.
- HIV: At least once to make sure of your HIV status.
- Depression: Men are often less in touch with their emotional health, so this is where a spouse can really help out. If your spouse has been down, sad, or feeling hopeless for two weeks or more, or if he or she has felt little interest or pleasure in doing things he or she once liked to do, the cause may be depression. Encourage your spouse to talk to a doctor about being screened for depression.

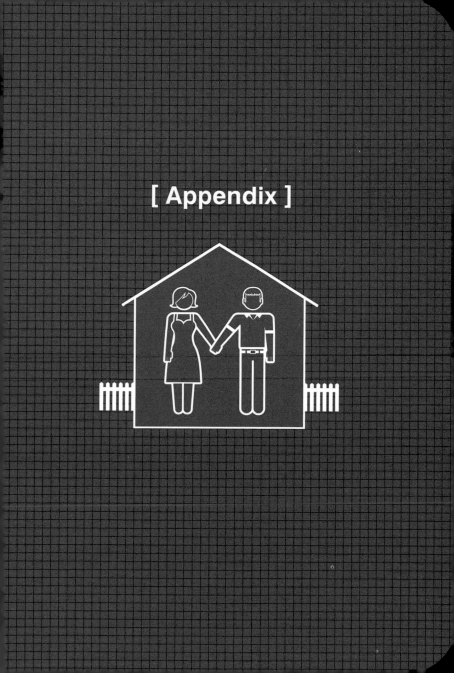

[Appendix]

Party Planning Checklist

ONE MONTH AHEAD
november 31

- [ ] Select date, time, and theme of party.
- [ ] Set budget.
- [ ] Prepare guest list.
- [ ] Send out invitations.

ONE TO TWO WEEKS AHEAD
december 18

- [ ] Plan your menu, décor, and music selections.
- [ ] Follow-up with those who have not RSVPed.
- [ ] Take inventory of party supplies and equipment. (Don't forget barware, matches, candles, liquor, table linens, utensils, serving plates and dishes, charcoal for grill and other party supplies and/or decorations.)
- [ ] Make your shopping list.
- [ ] Order cakes, appetizer platters, or any other food you are not preparing yourself.
- [ ] Shop for alcohol and nonperishable foods.

december 29 — TWO DAYS AHEAD

- [ ] Clean your house (including bathrooms).

- [ ] Start preliminary decorations.

december 30 — ONE DAY AHEAD

- [ ] Put out clean towels and a fresh roll of toilet paper.

- [ ] Buy perishable foods and last-minute items.

- [ ] Prepare nonperishable snacks.

- [ ] Set bar area and, if possible, table.

- [ ] Decorate your home.

december 31 — DAY OF THE PARTY

- [ ] Pick up ice, fresh flowers, and appetizer platters.

- [ ] Do a quick tidy up of house.

- [ ] Chill wine and drinks.

- [ ] Prepare food.

- [ ] Get showered and dressed.

- [ ] Set out appetizers, start music, and open wine (or put out other drinks).

- [ ] Welcome guests and get ready to have fun.

House Cheat Sheet

Number and Street

State/Province   **Zip/Postal Code**

DATE VISITED:
☐☐ / ☐☐ / ☐

ASKING PRICE:
$ ☐☐☐☐☐☐

Number and Street

State/Province   **Zip/Postal Code**

DATE VISITED:
☐☐ / ☐☐ / ☐

ASKING PRICE:
$ ☐☐☐☐☐☐

Number and Street

State/Province   **Zip/Postal Code**

DATE VISITED:
☐☐ / ☐☐ / ☐

ASKING PRICE:
$ ☐☐☐☐☐☐

Number and Street

State/Province   **Zip/Postal Code**

DATE VISITED:
☐☐ / ☐☐ / ☐

ASKING PRICE:
$ ☐☐☐☐☐☐

Number and Street

State/Province   **Zip/Postal Code**

DATE VISITED:
☐☐ / ☐☐ / ☐

ASKING PRICE:
$ ☐☐☐☐☐☐

NUMBER OF BEDROOMS: ☐ NUMBER OF BATHROOMS: ☐	INITIAL LIKES/DISLIKES:	QUESTIONS TO ASK:
NUMBER OF BEDROOMS: ☐ NUMBER OF BATHROOMS: ☐	INITIAL LIKES/DISLIKES:	QUESTIONS TO ASK:
NUMBER OF BEDROOMS: ☐ NUMBER OF BATHROOMS: ☐	INITIAL LIKES/DISLIKES:	QUESTIONS TO ASK:
NUMBER OF BEDROOMS: ☐ NUMBER OF BATHROOMS: ☐	INITIAL LIKES/DISLIKES:	QUESTIONS TO ASK:
NUMBER OF BEDROOMS: ☐ NUMBER OF BATHROOMS: ☐	INITIAL LIKES/DISLIKES:	QUESTIONS TO ASK:

Monthly Cooking Plan

	GROCERIES TO BUY		SUNDAY'S MEALS	MONDAY'S MEALS
WEEK 1		B:		
		L:		
		D:		
WEEK 2		B:		
		L:		
		D:		
WEEK 3		B:		
		L:		
		D:		
WEEK 4		B:		
		L:		
		D:		

TUESDAY'S MEALS	WEDNESDAY'S MEALS	THURSDAY'S MEALS	FRIDAY'S MEALS	SATURDAY'S MEALS

Romance

CHEAP DATES	GROUP DATES
Spend a day together at the beach.	Host a potluck dinner.
Volunteer for a cause you're both passionate about.	Go camping.
Explore a city or town on foot.	Compete in a couples' tournament of pool or mini golf.
Go to a free museum.	Visit a new bar for drin
Pack a picnic lunch and head to the park.	Go on a photo scaven hunt.

SPECIAL OCCASIONS

Re-create your first date.

Go on a romantic weekend getaway.

Eat at a nice restaurant you've both wanted to try.

Relax at a day spa.

Create a memory book of photos and keepsakes.

HOT-N-SPICY DATES

Visit the local adult sex-toy shop.

Give your spouse a sensual massage.

Rent an adult video.

Go skinny-dipping together.

Treat your spouse to a striptease.

Index

About the Author

CAROLINE TIGER is a freelance journalist and author of *How to Behave*, *How to Behave: Dating & Sex*, and *The Long-Distance Relationship Guide*. She lives in Philadelphia with her husband, Jonathan, and maintains that any resemblance between scenarios in this book and real life is entirely coincidental. Visit her online at www.carolinetiger.com.

About the Illustrators

PAUL KEPPLE and **SCOTTY REIFSNYDER** are better known as the Philadelphia-based studio **HEADCASE DESIGN**. Their work has been featured in many design and illustration publications, such as *AIGA 365* and *50 Books/50 Covers*, *American Illustration*, *Communication Arts*, and *Print*. Paul worked at Running Press Book Publishers for several years before opening Headcase in 1998. Paul graduated from the Tyler School of Art, where he now teaches. Scotty is a graduate of Kutztown University and received his M.F.A. from Tyler School of Art, where he had Paul as an instructor.

irreference \ir-'ef-(ə-)rən(t)s\ *n* (2009)

1 : irreverent reference
2 : real information that also entertains or amuses

How-Tos. Quizzes. Instructions.
Recipes. Crafts. Jokes.
Trivia. Games. Tricks.
Quotes. Advice. Tips.

Learn something. Or not.

VISIT IRREFERENCE.COM
The New Quirk Books Web Site